Date

CRIMES AGAINST WOMEN

ABOUT THE AUTHORS

Dr. William J. Bopp *is a criminologist and professor of Criminal Justice at Florida Atlantic University. A graduate of The University of California at Berkeley, he has written eight books, has been a consultant to scores of police departments and private corporations, and has testified often as an expert witness in civil suits that have been filed by women victimized by crimes. He has ten years police experience: five years with The Dade County, Florida, Public Safety Department; and five years with The Oakland, California, Police Department.*

Dr. James J. Vardalis *is a specialist in crime prevention and a member of the faculty at Florida Atlantic University in Fort Lauderdale, Florida. He has a doctorate in Public Administration and is a graduate of the National Crime Prevention Institute at The University of Louisville, The Robbery Prevention Program at The University of Delaware and The Texas Crime Prevention Institute. He has worked in the New Jersey State Prison at Rahway, and was a police officer for fifteen years: eight years with The Westfield and Stafford Township Police Departments in New Jersey; and seven years with The Fort Lauderdale Police Department, where as a crime prevention sergeant he conducted over 1,000 security surveys.*

Dr. Vardalis has also qualified as an expert in civil suits involving crimes against women in both federal and state courts.

CRIMES AGAINST WOMEN

DISCARD

By

WILLIAM J. BOPP

and

JAMES J. VARDALIS

CHARLES C THOMAS • PUBLISHER
Springfield • Illinois • U.S.A.

Published and Distributed Throughout the World by

CHARLES C THOMAS • PUBLISHER

2600 South First Street

Springfield, Illinois 62717

ISBN 0-398-05333-2

Library of Congress Catalog Card Number: 87-1896

With THOMAS BOOKS *careful attention is given to all details of manufacturing and
design. It is the Publisher's desire to present books that are satisfactory as to their physical
qualities and artistic possibilities and appropriate for their particular use.* THOMAS
BOOKS *will be true to those laws of quality that assure a good name and good will.*

Printed in the United States of America

SC-R-3

Library of Congress Cataloging-in-Publication Data

Bopp, William J.
    Crimes against women.

    Bibliography: p.
    Includes index.
    1. Women—United States—Crimes against. 2. Crime
and criminals—United States. 3. Crime prevention—
United States. I. Vardalis, James J. II. Title.
HV6250.4.W65B66   1987   362.8'8'088042   87-1896
ISBN 0-398-05333-2

12/88

CONTENTS

CRIMES AGAINST WOMEN

Chapter 1

INTRODUCTION: ON VICTIMOLOGY

Some years ago, the U. S. Department of Justice summarized the extent to which criminologists and researchers had been concerned with the study of crime victims and what could be expected in the future:

> Traditionally, both public attention and the criminal justice system have focused on criminal offenders. Criminal justice resources have been used to pursue, apprehend, judge, and imprison offenders and have paid little attention to their victims. Recently, however, public attention has turned to victims of crime as well. This new concern is reflected in legislation proposed or enacted at both State and National levels, in various service programs to aid victims and/or compensate them for financial losses, and in a greater sensitivity with the criminal justice system to the treatment of victims (either as victims or as witnesses). Within the academic community, too, the study of the victims of crime is emerging as a new field.

The focus of this work is on women as crime victims, with a collateral examination of crimes against children. Much of the data used in this book was collected by the Bureau of Justice Statistics (BJS) in its National Crime Survey, included in which was a victimization study. According the the BJS:

> In the past, our knowledge of the extent of crime came solely from persons who chose to report victimizations to the police. In the 1970's, the technique of victimization surveying was developed to learn about the impact of crime on victims through interviews with both victims and nonvictims in the general population. The Department of Justice began conducting a national victimization survey in 1973. This ongoing survey, known as the National Crime Survey, is sponsored by the Department's Bureau of Justice Statistics. The survey consists of interviews with a national sample of 60,000 households in which all members of the household are interviewed twice a year to determine whether they have been victims of crime. Crime victims are asked about the details of their victimization. Victimization surveys have also been conducted in a number of other countries throughout the world. By

3

focusing on the victim, these surveys have given impetus to the establishment of programs to ease the trauma of victimization.

The answer to "Who is a victim of crime?" may seem obvious. But it often isn't as easy to describe victims as one might suppose. For some crimes, such as rape or murder, of course, it is quite clear who has been victimized. But for other crimes, such as welfare or insurance fraud, embezzlement, public corruption, or vagrancy, the victim is less clearly defined. A crime in which corporate funds are taken may ultimately by paid for by shareholders. Welfare fraud is absorbed by taxpayers. Public corruption may affect the trust of the general public toward officeholders. For the crime of arson, the only official victim may be the owner of the building—for whom destruction may even by financially advantageous. If only the building is destroyed, perhaps the real victim is the insurance company that covers the loss (and ultimately all the policyholders whose premiums provided the funds). But in other cases, the lives or property of the building's tenants may be lost. For crimes of property, in general, the economic loss involved may be absorbed by the crime victim or may be covered partially or entirely by insurance. Defining the victims of crime can be more difficult that one might assume.

We have little or no data about the victims of some of the types of crime just described. The National Crime Survey, however, measures victimization for those crimes in which the victim can be clearly defined. The specific crimes covered in the survey are rape, robbery, assault, personal and household larceny, burglary, and motor vehicle theft. When a victimization is reported to the interviewer, whether of an individual (age 12 and over) or of a household, the survey obtains extensive information about the characteristics of the victimization. From this information we are learning more about the victims of crime than has ever been known before.

The relatively recent focus on crime victims has also led to rather well-defined justifications for this type of study. Consider the following from the U. S. Department of Health and Human Services:

Criminologists have traditionally concerned themselves with trying to find the *causes* of crime. Typically their concern is a matter of finding general answers to the question, "Why do crimes take place?" This search has led them to examine the antecedents and circumstances of various types of crime and the motivation of offenders, in the hope of explaining observed distribution of crimes in physical and social space, and variations in crime rates over time.

Until fairly recently, criminologists pursuing these questions tended to concentrate largely on persons who had committed crimes—a standard strategy being to compare criminals or delinquents (whether identified from official records or through observation or self-report methods) with noncriminals or nondelinquents, in the hope that the two groups would differ in some causally relevant ways. Thus it was often assumed, either implicitly or explicitly, that, for example, crimes of violence occurred because certain persons or classes of persons (the "dangerous classes") were exceptionally prone to use violence to settle disputes or attain other goals; these persons were then assumed to use violence against others who—so far as their role in the explanation of crimes was concerned—might just have happened to be standing there at the time. The criminal was thus typically conceived of as the "active" element in the situation and the victim as the wholly "passive" one.

Later and more sophisticated attempts to explain crime concentrated less on individual offenders and looked instead at the various social systems of which offenders were members or at the social control arrangements to which they were exposed. Explanations of these kinds referred to such things as disjunctions between societies' success-goals and the legitimate means of attaining those goals; to subcultural patterns of norms and values, and the methods by which these might be transmitted; to group processes in delinquent gangs; or to the situational absence of effective legal or moral controls on behavior. Even here, however, attention was generally on offenders or offenses, rather than on victims; it seems to have been generally assumed that the attributes and behavior of victims could in some sense be "averaged out" in the course of explaining the observed distribution of crimes and/or criminals.

In recent years, increasing attention has been paid to ways in which victims of crime (in the legal sense of that term) may play a part in the causation of crime. It has been noted that some kinds of people are especially vulnerable to crime and that they may, because of certain attributes or the nature of their interaction with offenders, be especially likely to become victims; in some cases, the person who is legally regarded as the victim of a crime may actually have caused that crime to happen. For certain types of crimes, at least, the probability of becoming a victim is not uniform but varies among different types of persons, groups, organizations, etc. To the extent that this is true, it is necessary to include some facts about the victims of crime in an adequate explanation of the spatial, temporal, or social distribution of crime. It is not clear how far this increased recognition of the victims' role in the causation of crime is due to changing fashions in criminological theory—to the popularity in recent years of interactionist theories, for example, and the brief flowering of the labeling perspective on deviance. But, whatever the reason, it is now clear that the behavior or attributes of victims need to be taken into account in explaining at least some types of crime. "Why do some people become victims of crime?" is not the same question as "Why do crimes take place?" But it may be necessary to answer the one in order to answer the other.

Some theories about victims' involvement in the causation of crime and research relevant to those theories are discussed elsewhere. At this point, we may note merely that such theoretical issues furnish one reason — a valid reason — for doing empirical research on victims and victimization. It also needs to be emphasized, however, that settling such questions of causation is not just an academic exercise. On the contrary, it has significant implications for public policy. For example, to what extent should the criminal law and the criminal justice system take account of the behavior of victims in inviting, negligently permitting, or otherwise facilitating crimes committed against them? It has recently been proposed in the Scandinavian countries that the owners of super-markets should no longer have the right to prosecute in cases of petty shoplifting, and it has been suggested that banks should themselves have to accept the responsibility for forged checks. The *policy* question at issue here is how far potential victims ought to have a duty to care, and how far, for example, stores may be treated as if they are provoking thefts by exhibiting goods in as tempting a way as possible. The related *empirical* question concerns the extent to which particular commercial practices — displaying goods in the open or cashing checks — tend to lead to the commission of crimes which would otherwise not take place.

One of the compelling questions which has arisen from crime victim studies is the extent to which people may contribute to their own vulnerability by placing themselves, either needlessly or unavoidably, in potentially perilous situations in which victimization is foreseeable. Accordingly, a number of researchers have begun to address this topic, including Gottfredson, whose lifestyle/exposure model is summarized below from a National Institute of Justice monograph:

> A number of researchers have concerned themselves with the etiology (or causes) of victimization and the critical dimensions that a theory or model of victimization would possess. Gottfredson's lifestyle/exposure model represented one attempt to explicate the etiology of criminal victimology in some tentative theoretical fashion. Gottfredson's model is essentially inductive. Based on evidence from the NCS (and other research) indicating consistent relationships between certain demographic characteristics (e.g., age, race, marital status) and the probability of victimization, it is posited that probablistic exposure and its antecedents — more importantly, lifestyle — determine the likelihood of victimization.
>
> Thus, in terms of Gottfredson's model, the reason that single individuals would be more likely to be victimized than married individuals would be that the lifestyle of singles is more likely to place them with high-risk times, places, and people. With respect to this model, empirical progress depends on identifying systematic relationships between various time-space-person coordinates and the probability of victimiza-

tion, and identifying those properties or characteristics of persons or objects that are predictive of these coordinates.

Some evidence for a lifestyle/exposure model has been provided which indicates systematic relationships between changes over time in patterns of routine activities (or lifestyle) and specific crime rates, and between personal characteristics, victim-offender relationships, and certain places and times and victimization rates. Hindeland et al. offered a series of propositions relating dimensions of lifestyle to the probability of exposure (and, thus victimization). In essence, Gottfredson recommended that further research be conducted which more directly tests the hypothesized relationships between various characteristics and operationalized measures of lifestyle and exposure.

The purpose of this book is to focus on one type of crime victim: women. In it are contained chapters on crimes which either victimize women exclusively or with great frequency (e.g., rape) or which present special problems to women (e.g., household burglary). While this is not a traditional crime prevention book it is anticipated that knowledge of the nature, extent and characteristics of some types of crime is a first step in deterring criminal activity.

BIBLIOGRAPHY

Bureau of Justice Statistics, *Victims of Crime.* Wash: U. S. Department of Justice, 1981.

Hindeland, M., M. Gottfredson and J. Garofolo, *Victims of Personal Crime.* Cambridge, MA: Balunger, 1978.

U. S. Department of Health and Human Services, *Research on Victims of Crime.* Rockville, MD: U. S. Department HHS, 1981.

U. S. Department of Justice, *Victims of Crime.* Wash: U. S. Department of Justice, 1981.

Chapter 2

RAPE

Some years ago, during the fledgling stages of scholarly inquiry into the crime of rape, a celebrated psychiatrist claimed that "He who cannot bite cannot kiss," an obtuse comment on his belief that male sexuality is often associated with aggressiveness and the urge to dominate, the exert power and control over a woman. While this generalization, like most, may be selectively accurate, and much too simple to be wholly true, it does reflect the starting point of most studies of causation: male aggression is a primary causitive factor in rape.

Rape is a crime which is both detested and misunderstood. Indeed, it should be loathed, not simply because of its violative nature and physical toll, but for the immense psychological damage and lingering emotional distress that it exacts from its victims. Nevertheless, rape need not and should not be misunderstood, since knowledge is a first step toward prevention. Accordingly, it will do well to first discuss rape as an historical phenomenon, before preceeding with a full-scale examination of this most troubling topic.

A Summary History

In contemporary America, rape is perceived as a form of deviant behavior, a socially unacceptable act. This perception contrasts dramatically with that of early civilizations, in which rape was a common practice, ratified by many societies as a prerogative of men, a way in which they validated their superiority over women.

According to Susan Brownmiller, whose book about rape, *Against Our Will,* has become a classic, abduction and rape were often employed by men in the courtship of women, even in otherwise civilized societies such as Fifteenth-Century England, in which so-called "bride capture" was a perfectly acceptable first step in the marriage ritual.

Warfare further reinforced this precept, as conquering armies viewed foreign women as part of the spoils of war, to be raped at will, an act well within the rules of warfare. Greece, Sparta and Rome all accepted and employed this practice. According to Brownmiller, even when rape was outlawed as a criminal act, it was still widely practiced and rarely punished, as evidenced by the Russian march into Berlin in World War II, during which rape was permitted, perhaps even encouraged, as a form of retribution against the hated Germans. In short, rape historically was a priviledge reserved for the winning side.

Rape was conspicuously ignored by early law. It was finally declared illegal, not because of a moral awakening on the part of male-dominated societies, but as an outgrowth of rapidly changing economic systems in which the rape of a virgin made her practically useless for marriage, thereby depriving her father of a substantial dowry. Rape, then, was an economic crime, not an interpersonal assault, for it was the father not the daughter who was the victim.

A woman's status was simple: she was either a betrothed virgin, who resided in the home of her parents; or she was a wife living in her husband's house. In effect, she had no independent status as a human being and the law tracked and strengthened these narrow social roles. If a man raped a virgin, he would be put to death. If he raped a married woman, his punishment was also death, but the woman was, despite the attack, an adulteress, according to early codified law, and could only be spared from death if her husband decided to intervene. A father who sexually assaulted his daughter would merely be banished from the community, to whom he was more of an embarrassment than a villian.

During the early years of the American democracy, rape was a crime in every state. Unhappily, slaves and Indians, who held no legal standing as persons, were notable exceptions to this legal protection, though males in these groups were held fully accountable for sexual assaults on white women. A plantation owner who raped a slave woman or a cavalry officer who sexually assaulted a "savage" were of little interest to the authorities. Conversely, blacks or Indians who victimized white women were guilty of atrocities, and often the subject of swift punishment, usually death, sometimes without the benefit of trial. Intraracial (black or Indian) rape was treated as an event unworthy of governmental intervention.

In Twentieth-Century America, long after the West had been settled and slavery had been abolished, the state statutes on rape were, theoretically, applicable to all citizens, regardless of race, economic status or social position. Nevertheless, in the hands of police officers, judges, and jurors, most of whom were white men, the application of these laws reflected the prejudices of middle-class America, a form of rough justice for victims. White men who were accused of raping white women were often acquitted, if during the cross-examination of their victims, which were usually permitted with little judicial interference, they could "discredit" their accusers. White men who raped black women were rarely charged, and almost never convicted when brought to trial. Black-on-black rapes were not generally police investigative priorities, and when trials were held and convictions were secured, penalties were normally lenient. When, however, black men were accused of raping white women, the wheels of justice moved swiftly, with consistent "guilty" verdicts and maximum penalties—frequently death. These disparate outcomes contributed to eventual U. S. Supreme Court actions which struck down state capital punishment statutes.

Presently, there is a concerted attempt nationwide to uniformly apply the laws of sexual assaults. The emphasis is on prosecuting offenders, protecting victims and standardizing penalties. This growing emphasis on equal justice is a direct outgrowth of the contemporary feminism. In 1972, the country's first rape crisis center opened in Washington D.C., an historic occurrence in the anti-rape movement, and an innovation that has spread to virtually every state and most urban areas.

Nonetheless, myths and misconceptions still abound, including the assertion that a woman's mode of dress precipitates rape and that many rapes by acquaintences are civil rather than criminal matters.

Types of Rape

A high school girl and her date attend a Friday evening football game with friends, with whom they stop afterwards for a snack at a local fast food restaurant. At about eleven p.m. the gathering breaks-up and the couple, who live within ten blocks of one another, drive to a secluded area. The boy holds and kisses the girl, but when he attempts to become more amorous, she objects. He continues his advances and she resists, but he overpowers her. She is forced to have sexual intercourse with him, following which he sheepishly apologizes for getting "a little carried away." Although her clothes are wrinkled and slightly ripped, she has no visible signs of injury.

A forty-one year old divorcee ends her shift as a bartender at two a.m. on a Tuesday morning, gets in her car and drives home to a sprawling 600 unit rental apartment complex in a modest suburban community near a major city. Because of the hour, she is compelled to park some distance from her apartment, in the outer perimeter of the lot, which rings the cluster of 20 low rise buildings that encompass the premises. She parks the car, alights from it, then begins the long walk to her unit. The area is not well-illuminated. After a few steps, she sees a shadowy form out of the corner of her eye. She turns, just in time to feel a sharp, stunning blow to the temple, delivered by a lone man in dark clothing who had concealed himself behind a dumpster. He drags her between two cars, pummels her unmercifully, rapes her, then kicks her into unconsciousness. She is visibly and seriously injured, and requires hospitalization, major surgery and a lengthy period of psychological counseling.

Both of these incidents are real cases. Each are also rapes. Admittedly, the latter is a more brutal assault than the former but, nevertheless, both are rapes. Neither of the rapists was caught. In fact, the first rape was not even reported to the police. These cases illustrate the two generally recognized types of rape: *acquaintance rape;* and *rape by strangers.*

Acquaintance rape is, as the name denotes, an assault by someone who is known to the victim: a neighbor, a co-worker, a schoolmate, a friend. The earliest studies conducted of reported rapes indicated that this category was a significant problem. Menachem Amir, in his groundbreaking analysis of 646 forcible rapes in Philadelphia between 1958 and 1960, concluded that about half the victims in his study had been involved in some form of relationship with the offenders prior to the attack.

Authoritative contemporary studies do not completely support the early findings that acquaintance rape represents roughly half-or-more-of all rapes. Today, a woman is more than twice as likely to be attacked by a stranger than by a man she knows, as evidenced by national data on sexual assaults over a ten year period which concluded that 68 percent of all rapes and attempted rapes were committed by strangers, while 32 percent involved assailants known to the victim.

One of the major problems associated with acquaintance rape is the reluctance of victims to report their attacks to authorities. According to a U. S. Department of Justice study:

> ... a victim may be less likely to report a rape—either to the police or to a survey interviewer—when she knows her assailant than when he is a stranger. The victim may feel a greater sense of embarrassment under these circumstances. She may feel that she should have been able to prevent the attack. She may wish to protect the identity of the assailant who is a friend or family member. She may even fear reprisals or worry

that her account of the attack will not be believed. There is some support in the (rape) statistics for this line of reasoning.

Probably the most prevalent form of sexual assault by an acquaintance, excluding attacks on children, is so-called *date rape,* the subject of the initial case example discussed in this section. Date rape can be especially pernicious because victims often feel a measure of undeserved culpability in the attack and are frequently teenagers, who may have just begun to explore their sexuality and who find themselves caught in the confusing conflict between peer pressure and parental restrictions. On the last point, it is difficult enough to be a teenager in America without facing a sexual crisis alone, during the vulnerable years of adolescence, at a time when one may have difficulty coping with even the most routine problems associated with this period of development. The result can be profound psychological damage, a shattered self-concept, disgust, guilt, repression and an epic emotional setback which can lead to dire consequences for the victim. More of the emotional impact of rape may be found in Chapter 8.

There is a dearth of quality research on date rape, yet some studies have shed light on the phenomenom. As might be expected, an extraordinary number of these types of assault occur during the days and hours most closely associated with dating: weekends between 10:00 p.m. and 2:00 a.m. In a study of 71 college men who had admitted to engaging in date rape, Eugene J. Kanin found that almost all the assailants were products of "a highly erotic-oriented peer group" that emphasized sexual conquest, quantity over quality and aggressiveness over intimacy.

According to Kanin, most men (82 percent) had prior dates with the women they attacked, and they tended to feel that their victims had made "implicit (sexual) promises" that had been reneged on, thus leading to the assault. In trying to explain why they raped, the men made two points. First, they said, it was only after their dates had become extremely aroused sexually that they became forceful in the face of resistance, which the attackers believed was an insincere signal to be ignored.* Second, two-thirds of the men blamed excessive drinking as a major causitive element in their behavior. While not relieving men of the responsibility for their actions, Kanin arrived at a provocative

---

*A study of teenagers in Southern California found that more than half the boys and 42 percent of the girls thought that "forced sexual intercourse was permissable under certain circumstances."

conclusion: "One might point out that the female did play a part in her victimization by instituting high levels of exposure to risk."

In any event, women who have been assaulted on dates are *victims* in every sense of the word. While stranger rape is a despicable crime, victims of this form of assault are much more likely to receive the support and empathy of friends and family than date rape victims, who are not only physically attacked and emotionally damaged, but compelled to rethink their definition of trust, intimacy, loyalty, friendship and morality.

The most frightening and terrifying form of rape is assault by a complete stranger. It may be the single crime that women dread the most, and for good reason. The assailant is more likely to be armed in this type of encounter than in acquaintance rape. The victim stands a greater chance of being injured during the attack. She could very well be robbed as well as raped.

While a rather small number of rapists are sadistically violent, the publicity surrounding their grisly exploits contributes to the terror of rape. Consider the following passage from a criminology text:

> We know very little systematically about violent rapists. They constitute only a small portion of all sex offenders, but their acts are so violent at times that they result in homicide. When studied, violent sex offenders are often grouped with more conventional murderers and sex offenders. The violence inflicted by the rapist on his victim may involve slashing, strangling, and other forms of extreme violence. In some cases the violent sex offender may not have intercourse with his victim but, rather, may engage in other forms of sexual contact, or such may be combined with intercourse. The victims may be casual pickups or they may be taken entirely by surprise by the offender who appears in the victim's car, on the sidewalk, or in some other place.

The relatively recent exploits of serial rapist and murderer, Christopher Wilder, a sexual psychopath, are consistent with the above description. He would lure women into accompanying him on the pretext of being a professional photographer interested in introducing them to a career in modeling. He appeared normal—even professional—in every respect. Once alone with a woman, he would terrorize and rape her, usually mutilate and torture her, then kill her. The bodies of some of his victims were never found.

There is one notable case in which a woman whom Wilder stopped and talked to in a shopping mall but who refused to be entrapped by his subterfuge, rebuffed him and his enticements. She walked away, but was followed to her car in the parking lot by Wilder, who struck her with an incapacitating blow, then abducted her. She was taken across the state line, held captive in a motel room and brutally assaulted. She survived the ordeal and escaped, injured but alive. There are other instances in which women rejected the advances of Christopher Wilder but were neither attacked nor kidnapped by him because of the risk involved in attempting to do so from either populated or well secured premises.

It should be noted that, although rape is a reality in America, the statistical chances of a woman being victimized by this type of assault are very low, and the likelihood that, if encountered by a rapist he will be a sadistic Christopher Wilder-type, is quite rare. As with most crimes, the publicized descriptions of rapes are often extreme cases, sometimes sensationalized by the press. The next section should shed some light on the nature and extent of rape.

A Profile of Rape in America

The U. S. Department of Justice recently released a study of rape in America that was the result of sampling techniques in which citizens were interviewed to determine rates of victimization. As a consequence, the results depict an estimate of *actual* rapes, not just *reported* ones. Additionally, the analysis focused on both rapes and attempted rapes, which were defined as "... verbal threat of rape only." Most of the material which follows is from that study, which encompassed the years 1973 through 1982, and which represents the most illuminating profile of rape ever published.

Rape and attempted rape, for all their fearsome and brutal aspects, are relatively uncommon crimes compared with other violent crimes such as robbery or assault, accounting for about 3 percent of all violent crimes. In 1983, an estimated 154,000 rapes and attempted rapes occurred, or roughly one for every 600 females 12 years of age and over. Of those 154,000 cases, only 185 deaths associated with rape were reported, meaning that there was about one death for every 830 rapes or attempts.

The following figures depict rape in comparison with crimes in general and crimes of violence during the ten-year period:

Total Crime, Violent Crime and Rape (1973–1982)

	Number of Victimization	Annual Rate Per 1,000 Population
Total Crime	395,172,000	—
Total Violent Crime	59,050,000	—
Total Rape	1,634,000	0.93
Male Victims	123,000	.0.15
Female Victims	1,511,000	1.65
Attempted Rape	1,032,000	1.13
Complete Rape	479,000	0.52

For purposes of this section, the 123,000 rapes involving male victims will not be analyzed. The focus of attention here will be on the 1,511,000 rapes and attempts involving female victims.

Two-thirds of all rapes and rape attempts occur at night, with the largest proportion occurring between 6:00 p.m. and midnight. Rape attempts were twice as likely as completed rapes to occur during the daytime, meaning that would-be rapists are much more successful in achieving their goals in darkness than in daylight, for obvious reasons.

The site of rapes and rape attempts vary, but two diverse locations lead the list of settings, as reflected in the following table:

Places Where Rapes Occurred (1973–1982)

Percent of Rapes Occurring:	Total Rapes	Attempted Rapes	Completed Rapes
On the street, or in a park, playground, parking lot or parking garage	39%	43%	31%
At home	27%	24%	35%
Near home	7%	9%	4%
In a commercial building	5%	6%	3%
In school	2%	2%	
Other locations	20%	16%	27%

This is important data, for if you couple the darkness factor with the most common location of occurrence (street, park, playground, parking lot/garage), it is clear that a woman's vulnerability to rape can be decreased by avoiding certain places at certain times, or by taking special precautions when forced to be in high risk places during high crime hours.

With regard to the high percentage of rapes which occur "at home" it can be assumed that the term "home" really refers to two locations: the home of the victim, and that of the assailant. It is likely that most of the rapes and attempts that occurred in the assailant's home resulted after the victim voluntarily went there (acquaintance rape). Rapes which occurred in the victim's home were a combination of acquaintance rape, after the assailant was invited to visit, and rape by a stranger, in which the rapist gained entry through illicit means, either by deception or burglary.

Rape victims are young, with the highest victimization rates in the 16-to-24-year-old category. Young women in this age group were two to three times more likely to be victims than women as a whole, though 26 percent of rape victims were in the 25-to-34-year-old group. A striking 85 percent of all victims of *completed* rape were unmarried: single (57 percent), divorced (18 percent), separated (8 percent) or widowed (2 percent).

More than three-fourths of all rapes involve one victim and one offender. About 15 percent are lone victims attacked by more than one offender. In less than 10 percent of the incidents were there multiple victims.

Most offenders are unarmed, though weapons were either used or suspected in 36 percent of rapes, with the type of weapon together with the percentage of use listed below:

Weapon	Percent of Victimization With
Knife	12
Gun	10
Other	4
Unknown	1
Suspected	9

Many victims offered some form of resistance to assailants. Most women who resisted were victims of attempted rape, while most not using self-protection were victims of completed rape. Thus, resistence diminished the likelihood that the assault would be completed. Unfortunately, it also increased the victim's probability of injury. Consider the following tables:

Female Victims of Rape Using/Not Using Self-Protection (1973–1982)

	Number of Victims	Total	Attempted Rape	Completed Rape
All Victims	1,511,000	100%	68%	32%
Using Self-Protection	1,257,000	100%	73%	27%
Not using Self-Protection	254,000	100%	44%	56%

Female Victims of Rape by Use of Self-Protection and by Injury

	Total Numbers	Total %	Victims With Injury	Victims Without Injury
All Victims	1,043,000	100%	56%	44%
Using Self-Protection	872,000	100%	57%	43%
Not using Self-Protection	171,000	100%	47%	53%

Although the data collected in the study did not include the severity of injuries, it did list the nature. The most common physical injuries, in addition to the rape itself, were bruises, black eyes and cuts (31 percent), internal injuries or knocked unconscious (4 percent), and broken bones or teeth knocked out (2 percent). The cumulative cost of medical care for all the injured victims was more than $71 million or about $104 per victim.

The social stigma traditionally attached to rape makes the experience difficult for many victims to discuss. Only about half of the victims of rape or attempted rape surveyed during the decade reported the crime to the police. As might be expected, the rate was somewhat lower for attempted rape than for rape, and cases involving strangers were more readily reported than those involving acquaintances. According to victims, their experiences were reported to the police 58 percent of the time if the rape was completed and 50 percent of the time if the rape was attempted. Many victims who did not report the crime to the police gave more than one reason for not reporting. The most common reasons given, in order of frequency, included:

- Private or personal matter
- Nothing could be done
- Afraid of reprisal
- Reporting to someone else
- Police would not want to be bothered

- Didn't think it was important
- Didn't want to get involved
- Didn't want to take the time

Why Do Men Rape?

Theorists are often inclined to accept narrow explanations—the single-theory approach—of rape while rejected all other views, regardless of how persuasive they may be. For example, a psychiatrist might take the position that rape is a product of a diagnosable and treatable psychological disfunction in all cases, and the notion that a rapist merely wishes to dominate women is a by product of his disfunction not a causitive factor, while a prison social worker may become convinced that men with high testosterone levels are "driven" to rape and that drugs which diminish the drive are the answer. Both may be somewhat correct in their analyses of the narrow cross section of rapists with whom they deal; however, both are quite wrong in asserting that the 1.5 million rapes studied by the Justice Department had one single cause and one single cure. Rape is a complex crime committed by men who are often complicated people with a myriad of problems.

There are various explanations in the criminological literature of the causes of rape, but all seem to involve, in some way or another, the concept of aggression, where men either choose, are compelled to or are driven to sexually assault women. Yet, male aggression is a factor in art, literature, music, sports, entertainment, business and politics. So how can one explain why some men rape and others do not? The answer to this question is not as clear as it could be, but what is clear is that rape is a crime which involves both aggression and sexuality but that sexuality is more a method of expressing aggression than an urge to satisfy erotic yearnings.

What causes socially destructive forms of aggression in men has resulted in four different theoretical explanations of aggression, each of which merits attention. These theories are: (1) ethologistic theory; (2) reactive theory; (3) social learning theory; and (4) psychological theory.

Ethology is the study of innate behavior patterns in animals. *Ethologistic Theory* holds that many patterns of behavior are motivated by an internal drive, which operates quite independently of external environmental stimulation. These drives are instinctual and biologically triggered.

Some men perform antisocial acts because of this drive, this internal force which is directly related to aggression, according to this theory.

There have been some recent studies of the relationship of the male hormone testosterone to aggression. The studies offer conflicting findings. Some have found that young men with high levels of testosterone also exhibit high levels of hostility and aggression, as measured by standardized psychologic tests. Others have found that no such relationship exists. Both seem to agree, however, that if there is a correlation between testosterone levels and aggressive behavior it exists almost exclusively in younger men. With improvements in the techniques to measure the presence of testosterone in men, more work will undoubtedly be done in this area.

Some of the strongest proponents of testosterone as a cause of aggressive sexual behavior are professionals who work in prisons and state mental hospitals in which small numbers of convicted rapists have been administered drugs designed to lower their "sex drives." While the preliminary results of these endeavors have been reported as a valuable new behavior modification tool, the jury is still out on this approach.

In the 1920's, social scientists isolated frustration as the single most important factor in the expression of aggressive behavior. Over the years, the concept was developed into one of the most influential and persistent sociological theories on aggression: *The Reactive Theory*. Rejecting the ethologistic approach which rested on biological bases, the starting point of reactive theory was that aggression was, in all cases, caused by frustration. The theory went further.

Reactive philosophy asserts that: (1) variation in the amount of frustration, the strength of frustration and the number of frustrating experiences a man is exposed to are directly related to his tendency toward aggressive behavior; (2) the inhibition of an act of aggression varies with the strength and certainty of punishment; (3) most acts of aggression caused by frustration are aimed at the person (*or their substitute*) perceived to be the source of frustration; and (4) the expression of an act of aggression serves as a type of catharsis which reduces, at least temporarily, the need to engage in further aggressive behavior.

A major element in *Social Learning Theory* is that aggressive behavior is often instantly rewarding. Criminals, for example, whether they are armed robbers or rapists, usually stand a statistically good chance of avoiding capture, so their acts may well be looked on as successful

goal-directed behavior. According to Albert Bandura, a leading propo-
nent of this theory:

> In the social learning analysis of motivation, incentives constitute
> important impellers of action. A great deal of aggression is prompted
> by its anticipated benefits. Here the instigator is the pull of expected
> success rather than the push of aversive treatment.

Bandura contends that behavior is learned by observation of models.
Thus, children who witness aggressive behavior, especially if those acts
involve people they admire, are most likely to engage in aggressive
behavior themselves. A good deal of research has been conducted on this
notion, and much of it concerns the impact of mass media, especially
television, on children. The findings indicate that T.V. furnishes male
children have an almost endless supply of aggressive, violent role models
to emulate, and that children do imitate these aggressive models.
'Social learning theory is somewhat consistent with a feminist view of
rape which holds that men are not innately more violent than women
but they are nonetheless more predisposed toward violence because of
conditions in society which promote male aggressiveness while encouraging female passivity and acquiescence.' These culturally reinforced stereotypes have led to sexism, inequality and a society that accepts as inevitable
male violence and female victimization. Laws and their enforcement
may be an important element in making rape a manageable problem,
but central to any long-term solution is a profound change in the traditional societal views of male dominance and female submissiveness.

The final approach to be discussed is the *Psychological Theory*, which
subdivides aggression into two major types: active aggression, in which a
person wishes to harm, to dominate or to destroy an object; or passive
aggression, the wish to be dominated, harmed or destroyed. Unacceptable
behavior resulting from aggression, according to this theory, always
stems from a psychological problem, that usually can be diagnosed,
treated and cured.

Nicholas Groth, in a study of convicted sex offenders, developed a
working typology of rapes which is consistent with the psychological
theory. To Groth, there are three patterns of rapes. First, there is *anger
rape*, in which pent-up bitterness, hostility and rage is discharged against
a victim. The force used in the attack is often excessive, since the rapist
wishes to inflict as much pain as possible on his victim. The rape is
usually a spontaneous act arising out of a personal setback the attacker

has just experienced. The second category is *power rape,* by a man who needs to dominate, to exercise control over a woman in order to prove his sexual potency or to somehow put to rest, at least temporarily, his sexual or personal insecurities. He will try to achieve his objectives with minimal force inasmuch as his goal is not punishment but dominance. He is out to validate his virility. In *sadistic rape,* the attacker wants to destroy his victim. He will employ torture, degradation and humiliation to achieve his ends. He may select victims who exhibit the personal traits he despises most, traits which remind him of earlier experiences with women he feared or hated (mother, girlfriend, ex-wife, etc). If he nurtures a hatred of women in general, the rapist may be less selective in his choice of victims. Of course, this is the most dangerous type of rapist; fortunately it is also the rarest. Groth has been recognized as a major contributor to the concept that rape is not a sexual crime, it is a crime of violence which employs sexual means.

It seems appropriate to close this section with a quote from a social scientist who had just evaluated an experiment that concluded with a less than balanced theory of crime:

> Experiments such as these have demonstrated the complex interrelationships of the determinants of aggressive behavior and the danger of attributing everything to a single factor.

On a Fourth Category of Rape: The Opportunist

Groth has developed and others have accepted the three category typology of rapists, to the extent that it has become dogma in the field. The centerpiece of these three patterns has been previously stated: rape is not a sexual crime; it is a crime of aggression using sexual means. Thus, rapists either choose or are driven to rape through anger, the need to exert power, or sadism.

It is suggested here, that some rapists *are* in fact motivated, not by complicated emotional or societal forces, but by pure sexuality. This sexuality may be an impulse, a drive, a compulsion or a physical need; however, it seems reasonable that, at least in some men, the need for a sexual outlet, possibly coupled with the excitement of unsanctioned behavior, leads to a form of rape which transcends the three traditional categories attributed to *all* rapists. This type of rapist, then, is an *opportunist* who may become involved in date/acquaintance assault or, if circumstances allow, stranger rape.

The data which exists on sexual assaults on men by men (12,000 annually according to the BJS) seems to indicate that Groth's typology of rapists may be incomplete, especially if assailants are bi-sexual or are those who engage in same sex assaultive behavior only in institutional settings (e.g., jail, prison, etc.), and have relatively "normal" sex lives elsewhere.

If *opportunistic* rapists do exist, and they are not driven by the three forces described by Groth, then such a new category has profound meaning for prevention, detection, diagnosis, treatment and rehabilitation.

Because of feminist acceptance of the premise that rapists are fundamentally compelled by forces other than sex drive (i.e., power, anger, sadism) and that sex is a device to exploit women rather than an end in itself, an addition to Groth's typology may meet with some resistance. Nevertheless, the author believes that there is reason to believe that some rapes are purely sexual crimes, devoid of the complex motivational and societal factors which have been associated with rapists. In any event, it is time to revisit Groth's working typology of rapists. Since contemporary theory does not seem to adequately explain the entire rape phenomenon.

Rape of Elderly Women

Rape of elderly women is very rare. Only about three percent of all rapes involve victims over the age of fifty. But, that still means that between 4,000 and 5,000 older women are sexually assaulted annually. The nature of these assaults differs dramatically from similar cases involving younger women or rape victims in general. Some of the most persuasive studies of elderly rape involved clinical interviews and case file evaluations of offenders in correction institutions or treatment centers. One such study, published by Groth and Birnbaum, collected information on 170 assailants who had raped adult women over a five year period of time, thirty of whom had selected women substantially older than them and twenty of whom had chosen as victims women over fifty years of age.

According to Groth and Birnbaum, the assailants were generally young, white and single. The average age of offenders was about twenty-three; fifty-two percent of victims were over sixty. The family life of offenders was revealing. Most had early and continuing developmental problems as children: problems in school, in primary relationships, at home. The quality of their home life was dismal, with absent or "psychologically absent" fathers. In those home where the father was present, the interaction between parents was often characterized by conflict and it was not unusual for a father to be an alcoholic or physically abusive or "cruel." In effect, fathers were undependable and unreliable men who were unfaithful to their wives and disinterested in their children. Mothers were domineering, manipulative, overprotective and promiscuous. Love an warmth were absent commodities in these homes. None of the offenders had a happy home life as a child.

Fifty-two percent of the victims were sexually assaulted in their own homes and twenty-four percent were attacked in their cars, a pattern which conflicts dramatically with that of younger victims. Almost eighty percent of the assaults were by strangers.

Probably the most striking aspect of the rape of elderly women was the extent to which the victims were seriously injured during the attack. While a little more than one-half of all women who are sexually assaulted are injured, and their injuries are primarily bruises and cuts, sixty percent of the elderly women were very seriously injured or killed. Forty-three percent were sadistically beaten, seven percent were stabbed and ten percent were murdered. In short, considerably more physical force was employed by offenders than was needed to overcome a victim's opposition, which was often feeble at best. Almost two out of every three offenders were armed, usually with a knife. Eighty-one percent of the rapes were completed.

Immediately prior to the assaults, most offenders who were interviewed admitted that they were in the throes of an extremely agitated emotional state: stress, anger, depression, usually brought on by an event involving an important woman in the assailant's life, such as a mother, wife, sister or girlfriend. Half of the men described the attack as unplanned and spontaneous.

It is painfully clear that the sexual assault of elderly women, while uncommon, offers a more substantial threat to life and limb than the rape of younger victims. This peril is not as much related to the greater propensity of the elderly to sustain injuries that more youthful persons would avoid under the same conditions as it is to the sadistic bent of offenders who seek out older victims. In effect, these men are not content to have their way sexually, they are only satisfied by lashing out physically against one of the most vulnerable groups in America.

Trends in Law

Every civilized society establishes norms for the regulation of sexual behavior. In contemporary western civilization, the most universally accepted norm is that sexual relations between a man and a woman must be by mutual consent. In America, this norm is not only a behavioral guideline, it is a law that contains harsh sanctions for disobedience, but which cannot be applied *unless the crime is reported.*

Rape is generally perceived by people as "carnal knowledge of a female forcibly and against her will," which is both the historical and common law definition. However, there are various other related crimes that make this rather narrow definition somewhat outmoded. For instance, there is so-called "statutory rape," sexual relations between an adult and a minor; sexual relations between a person and a victim who has been drugged; rape of a male; and sexual relations with an incapacitated or mentally defective victim. As a way of consolidating these and other related offenses into a single statute many states have done away with the traditional rape designation and grouped these unlawful activities under the title of either "sexual assault" or "sexual battery," with appropriate definitions and varying penalties based on the severity of the attack, or the age of the victim (e.g. under twelve-years old), or if the assailant was armed.

Over the past ten years, many state sexual assault statutes have been revisited and reevaluated by lawmakers as a reaction to criticism that provisions were not victim-oriented. For example, there is a movement away from the requirement that a victim's testimony about her assault must be correborated, either by another person or by an investigating police officer who was on the scene shortly after the attack. Following is an excerpt from a state statute with a modified corroboration provision:

> The testimony of the victim need not be corroborated in prosecutions; however, the court may instruct the jury with respect to the weight and quality of the evidence.

Other changes in law have also been made in an attempt to protect victims from rough justice without sacrificing the rights of defendants. One of the most controversial aspects of rape trials has always been the abuse of a victim during cross examination, especially in the area of prior sexual relations. Historically, the victim's past including her sexual past, was fair game, with the courts permitting almost unrestricted questioning by defense attorneys, inquiries which were not only traumatic and demeaning, but which often tended to prejudice juries against victims. Moreover, fear of abusive cross-examinations dissuaded many women from reporting their assaults to the police. A number of states have moved to prohibit or restrict such inquiry, as evidenced by the following excerpt from a state sexual battery law:

> Specific instances of prior consensual sexual activity between the victim and any person other than the offender shall not be admitted into evidence in prosecutions; however, when consent by the victim is at issue, such evidence may be admitted if it is first established by the court outside the presence of the jury that such activity shows such a relation to the conduct involved in the case that it tends to establish a pattern of conduct or behavior on the part of the victim which is relevant to the issue of consent.

The movement to make sexual assault statutes more sensitive to the special problems of rape victims is continuing, as well it should. Yet, the problems associated with rape trials are only partially related to statutory language. Regardless of how flawless a law may be, it can be subverted by judges harboring traditional misconceptions about the nature of rape or the culpability of innocent victims. News accounts of judges who blame, either directly or indirectly, a rape victim for her own assault because of her manner of dress, or for being "provocative" or because she was out late and unescorted, still appear with disturbing regularity. In spite of that, the trend is toward better laws and the even-handed administration of justice.

Conclusion

The historical status of rape has evolved from a socially acceptable form of courtship in early societies to a despised type of deviance punished by lengthy prison sentences in contemporary America. The past ten-to-fifteen years have seen some remarkable changes in the ways in which society and its institutions perceive and treat rape victims, largely because of harsh and justified criticism by women's organizations of the absence of victim support systems, the dearth of good data on the nature and extent of rape, the flaws in state sexual assault statutes and the demeaning treatment victims have suffered at the hands of a criminal justice system which was supposed to protect them. As a consequence, the most comprehensive study of rape in history has been conducted, the results of which have shed an enormous amount of light on the crime, its victims and offenders; studies continue—and theories abound—on the question of what motivates rapists; legal changes have strengthened and made laws more victim-oriented; victim treatment and advocacy programs have become the norm, especially in urban areas; and "traditional" attitudes on rape seem to be changing.

Much has been done in a rather short period of time after centuries of neglect and ignorance; much more needs to be done, especially on myths and outmoded public perceptions of rape victims. But, for the first time in history, a real anti-rape movement of consequence exists that promises to consolidate the reforms presently in place while pressing for needed changes in the future, for the ultimate goal is not innovation, it is *prevention.*

BIBLIOGRAPHY

Amir, Menachem, *Patterns in Forcible Rape.* Chicago: University of Chicago Press, 1971.

Brownmiller, Susan, *Against Our Will: Men, Women and Rape.* New York: Simon and Schuster, 1975.

Goldberg, Steven, *The Inevitably of Patriarchy.* New York: William Morrow, 1974.

Groth, A. Nicholas and Jean Birnbaum, *Men Who Rape.* New York: Plenum Press, 1979.

Hicks, Dorothy J., "Rape: Sexual Assault" in *American Journal of Obstetrics and Gynecology.* Vol. 137, No. 8, August 15, 1980, pp 931–935.

Kanin, Eugene J., "Date Rape: Unofficial Criminals and Victims". in *Victimology: An International Journal.* Vol. 9, November, 1984, pp 95–108.

Klaus, Patsy A. and Marshall DeBerry, "The Crime of Rape" in *Bureau of Justice Statistics Bulletin.* Washington: U. S. Department of Justice, 1985.

McDermott, M. Joan, *Rape Victimization in 26 American Cities.* Washington: U. S. Government Printing Office, 1979.

Nettler, Gwynn, *Killing One Another.* Cincinnati: Anderson Publishing, 1982.

Reid, Sue Titus, *Crime and Criminology,* 2nd ed. New York: Holt, Rinehart and Winston, 1979.

Siegel, Larry J., *Criminology.* St. Paul: West Publishing, 1983.

Chapter 3

FAMILY VIOLENCE

While it may be overly melodramatic to say that family violence has reached "epidemic proportions," it is certainly accurate to suggest that, from all the respectable contemporary research studies available on the issue, there seems to be a profound and growing problem of violent behavior in the American family, whose members are both assailants and victims of this distressing phenomenom.

There are a myriad of aspects of family violence, some of which are covered in other chapters of this book. The focus of attention in this chapter, however, will be on three distinct areas: wife abuse, child battering and elderly abuse.

Wife Abuse

Consider the following passage from an authoritative book on the topic by Barden and Barden:

> Violence against wives is a crime of enormous proportions. It occurs in families from all racial, economic, and religious backgrounds ... Battered women with few economic resources are more visible because they seek help from public agencies; however, middle and upper class women also seek refuge and assistance, although more often in hotels and from private agencies.

According to studies of the problem, some two million wives are severely assaulted by their husband each year. This form of violence occurs at least once in two-thirds of *all* marriages. The battering may very well escalate in severity over time, to the extent that fully thirty percent of female homicide victims are murdered by their husbands or boyfriends.

The U. S. Department of Health and Human Services has addressed the subject and the following has been reprinted from one of its publications.

Wife Abuse: The Facts

Instances of wife abuse have been on record in the United States since the 1830s, but only every now and then does it arouse public concern. Generally, public opinion supports traditional family relations and male authority. The battering syndrome is both cause and effect of stereotyped roles and the unequal power relations between men and women. No social class is exempt. Wife abuse occurs in wealthy and working class families. Over the years it has been tolerated by those who govern community affairs, the courts, medicine, psychiatry, police, schools, and the church. History shows that the helping professional often protected patterns of family authority, unwittingly sanctioning wife abuse rather than condemning it.

Defining wife abuse or wife battering is not easy. For starters, whom are we thinking of when we use the word "wife?" Actually, any woman who maintains an intimate relationship with a man (her husband, ex-husband, boyfriend or lover) could become a battered or abused "wife." The words "abused" or "battered" which are used here do not refer to the normal conflict and stress that occur in all close relationships, but rather to the violence that can cause serious injury or death. In the pamphlet, "Assaults on women: rape and wife-beating," Natalie Jaffe cites a typical description of the kind of physical harm suffered by battered women surveyed in shelters and treatment in California.

"Most injuries were to the head and neck and, in addition to bruises, strangle marks, black eyes, and split lips, resulted in eye damage, fractured jaws, broken noses, and permanent hearing loss. Assaults to the trunk of the body were almost as common and produced a broken collarbone, bruised and broken ribs, a fractured tailbone, internal hemorrhaging, and a lacerated liver." These are serious consequences of serious assaults. Another serious aspect is that once wife beating occurs, it is likely to happen again and again, with violence getting worse over time.

A woman who has been abused over a long period of time is afraid. Not only is she afraid that she, herself, will be seriously hurt, but, if she has children, she fears for their safety also. Her feelings of fear link her to all other women, from all classes of society, in similar situations.

Fear might be a woman's first and most immediate feeling during or after a beating, but other negative feelings may surface when she is not in physical danger. The abused woman is apt to develop doubts about herself. She might wonder if she is justified in fearing for her life and calling herself an "abused wife." Most likely, however, a woman who thinks or feels she is being abused, probably is.

Or, she may feel guilty, even though she's done nothing wrong. An abused wife may feel responsible for her husband's violence because in some way she may have provoked him. This has her placing the shame and blame on herself—instead of her abuser. The longer she puts up with the abuse and does nothing to avoid or prevent it, the less she likes herself. Along with the feeling of being a failure, both as a woman and in her marriage, may come a real feeling of being trapped and powerless, with no way out.

Present-day society is one in which violence in the movies, on TV, and in the newspapers is familiar and accepted. Many husbands who abuse their wives have learned that violence, especially against women, is okay. They often were abused themselves as children or saw their mothers abused. The battered wife most likely grew up in a similar environment.

There are other psychological reasons. A wife abuser tends to be filled with anger, resentment, suspicion, and tension. He, also, underneath all his aggressive behavior, can be insecure and feel like a loser. He may use violence to give vent to the bad feelings he has about himself or his lot in life. Home is one place he can express those feelings without punishment to himself. If he were angry with his boss and struck him, he would pay the price. But all too often he gets away without penalty when he beats his wife. She becomes the target of his vengeance, and he gets the satisfaction he's looking for.

What about the victimized wife? If she accepts her husband's traditional male authority, she may be labeled as immature. If she fights back or if she refuses to sleep with him if he's drunk, she might be accused of being hostile, domineering, and masculine. These are complaints of abused women.

Familiar patterns of wife abuse often develop in three phases: the tension-building phase, the explosion or the actual beating phase, and the loving phase. The tension builds over a series of small occurrences such as a wife's request for money, her refusal to do all the household chores without her husband's help, her serving a meal not pleasing to him, or similar incident. What follows is inevitable. She may become the object of any or all of the following assaults: punching with fists, choking, kicking, knifing, slamming against a wall, throwing to the floor, or shoving down the stairs. Sometimes even threats with a gun have been reported. When the beating is over, the couple move into the third phase. The batterer feels guilty about what he has done. He is sorry and may become loving towards her. He assures his wife that he will never do anything violent or hurtful to her again. At that moment, he may believe he will never hurt her again. She wants to believe him, hoping that he will change. However, even with professional help, the tension building and the beatings may continue.

Women have learned that it may be their own feelings of fear, guilt, or shame that keep them in a relationship that is physically abusive. Often, social and economic pressures compel a woman to stay. Sometimes she stays for lack of somewhere to go for shelter and advice or because she still feels that she loves her husband and that he might change, if only she can "hang in there." Tragically, in most cases, the abuse continues, for in fact her husband's behavior has nothing to do with her actions.

Other reasons for staying with him may seem as compelling. A woman may feel that a divorce is wrong and that she feels that her children need a father. She may be isolated with no outside job and few friends. The friends and relatives she does talk to may give her little support, perhaps because her situation frightens them and they don't want to admit to themselves that such violence could occur. If she confides in a counselor, she may also be encouraged to "save the marriage." And, along with her emotional dependence, she may worry about being able to find a job to support herself and her children. If she has her husband arrested, he may not be able to support her. If she doesn't have him arrested, he may beat her even more severely for trying to leave him. Is there a way out? Most women suffer these attacks for years before they finally find the courage and determination to take steps to keep from being victims of further abuse.

The first step for a woman to take is to admit to herself that she is being abused and that she is not being treated fairly. She has the right to feel safe from physical harm, especially in her own home.

A woman can do a number of things to protect herself. She can hide extra money, car keys, and important documents somewhere safe so that she can get to them in a hurry. The phone number of a police department should be handy. She should have a place to go, such as an emergency shelter, a social service agency, or the home of a trusted friend or relative.

During an actual attack, the woman should defend herself as best she can. As soon as she is able, she should call the police and get their names and badge numbers in case she needs a record of the attack. Most importantly, she should leave the house and take her children with her. She may need medical attention, too, because she might be hurt more severely than she realizes. Having a record of her injuries, including photographs, can protect her legally should she decide to press charges.

A woman needs to talk to people who can help. Good friends can lend support and guidance. Organizations that are devoted to women's concerns and not bound by society's traditions can assist her. They might help her explore her options in new ways. Emergency shelters for women, hotlines, women's organizations, social service agencies, community mental health centers, and hospital emergency rooms are all possible sources of support.

Above all, a woman has to determine her own best course of action. Positive measures such as confiding in a relative, talking seriously with a friend, or consulting with a counselor are steps in the right direction. With the help of informal and formal help sources, including individual counseling for the husband as well as herself, a woman may be able to bring an end to the problem.

It has been observed that abused women need to develop better feelings about themselves—that is, change their self-image. In a book, "Stopping Wife Abuse," by Jennifer Baker Fleming, the following attitudes are suggested as positive and useful:

- I am not to blame for being beaten and abused.
- I am not the cause of another's violent behavior.
- I do not like it or want it.
- I do not have to take it.
- I am an important human being.
- I am a worthwhile woman.
- I deserve to be treated with respect.
- I do have power over my own life.
- I can use my power to take good care of myself.
- I can decide for myself what is best for me.
- I can make changes in my life if I want to.
- I am not alone. I can ask others to help me.
- I am worth working for and changing for.
- I deserve to make my own life safe and happy.

Since there is no one cause of wife abuse, there is no easy way to prevent it. Until society rejects its tolerance and acceptance of violence for resolving conflict and expressing anger, meaningful changes in family relationships will not occur. Prevention starts with people changing their attitudes toward violence and women. No one deserves to be beaten or physically threatened, no matter what the excuse. It is a crime to beat anyone—a stranger, a friend, or your wife—and the law should be enforced. The tolerance of family violence as a way of life in one generation encourages family violence in another generation. Since the wife abuser didn't learn to deal with anger appropriately as a child, he handles his frustrations through aggression. He needs to know that it's human to feel anger, but inhuman to release those feelings by beating others. By learning to deal with those emotions through acceptable behavior, he can gain respect for himself and others. It's another positive step towards developing mutual respect in the husband-wife relationship where each sees the other as a worthy human being.

Child Battering

Historically, children were considered to be the property of their parents and, except in the most extreme cases, what they did with and to their offspring was no one's business but the family's. As a consequence, various forms of abusive behavior toward youngsters were, in most societies, not only widespread, they were culturally reinforced parental prerogatives, a form of normative behavior which was universally accepted by citizens.

The notion that a child was virtually its parents' chattel indicates why the historical ledger reflects atrocities ranging fron infanticide to abandonment, mutilation to child labor. In America, one of the first highly publicized instances of child maltreatment was the "Mary Ellen" case, in which New York City authorities, unable to find a law to arrest the youngster's parents for extreme physical cruelty, inasmuch as young children held no legal status as people, charged Mary Ellen's mother and father with cruelty to an animal, since Mary Ellen could only be protected as an animal if she was not a human being—by legal standards. The case, an embarrassment to the New York criminal justice system, led to the nation's first law on child abuse, a statute that was in time emulated by every state.

Perhaps the most important contemporary event in the evolution of a child abuse literature, was a speech by pediatrician C. Henry Kempe, when at a medical symposium he proposed the term "battered child syndrome" to direct attention to the seriousness of the problem. The term captured the imagination of the medical community and social scientists, who were persuaded that it was a phenomenon worth studying.

One of the first and most respected studies of child abusers was conducted by Steele and Pollock of the University of Colorado School of Medicine. In that classic study of sixty child abusers, it was discovered that they exhibited a single, universal characteristic that was identified as an important factor in both the early diagnostic process and in the treatment phase. According to Steele and Pollock:

> Without exception in our study, there is a history of (abusers) having been raised in the same style which they have recreated in the pattern of rearing their own children. All (as children) had experienced . . . a sense of intense, pervasive, continuous demand from their parents. This demand was in the form of expectations of good, submissive behavior, prompt obedience, never making mistakes, sympathetic comforting of parental distress, and showing approval and help for parental actions. Such parental demands were . . . excessive, not only in degree but . . . in prematurity . . . performance was expected before the child was able to fully comprehend what was expected or how to accomplish it.

It was, then, this type of child rearing practice—premature demands, parental criticism, youthful failure to live up to unreasonable expectations—which led to the kind of emotional distresses that resulted in the physical abuse of children, and to a situation in which children raised in this environment would also be predisposed to be abusers.

The federal government's National Center on Child Abuse and Neglect has profiled the maltreatment of children and the following section is reprinted, with editorial adaption, from its findings.

This section describes the particular kinds of maltreatment situations encompassed by the study and summarized relationships between major forms of in-scope maltreatment and various child, family and perpetrator characteristics.

Physical assault is largely self-explanatory. The only distinction was whether or not the assault was known to have entailed use of an implement (e.g., lamp cord, stick, cigarette, flat iron) or foreign substance (e.g., non-accidental drowning, poisoning, scalding). As shown in Table 1, assaults not involving known use of implement or foreign substance (e.g., hitting with hand or fist, kicking, biting, throwing or unknown means of assault) were the most common. Although there were some injuries at all severity levels (including death), moderate injuries were by far the most common in both subcategories. In both, about 15 percent of in-scope children were judged to be in-scope on the basis of probable harm—that is, there was no direct evidence of injury but, from the nature of the acts and events, it was judged highly likely that observable injury had occurred.

In the area of sexual exploitation, subcategories reflect different kinds of acts. Evidence of actual penile penetration—whether oral, anal or genital, homosexual or heterosexual—was required in the intrusion subcategory. Except for promoting or permitting of prostitution, allegations that a parent had knowingly permitted a child to engage in voluntary sexual activity with someone other than an adult caretaker were not accepted. Molestation with genital contact involved acts where some form of actual genital contact had occurred but were there was no specific indication of intrusion. "Other and unspecified" was just that, unspecified "molestation" or "sexual abuse" or sexually exploitative acts not known to have involved actual genital contact (e.g., fondling of breasts or buttocks, exposure). Threatened or attempted sexual assault not involving actual physical contact were not included (see emotional abuse).

No evidence of injury was required in the first two subcategories; circumstantial or direct evidence of moderate or greater injury was required in the third. In effect, it was accepted as a matter of definition that sexual exploitation involving intrusion or molestation with genital contact is inherently traumatic and injurious. For other kinds of acts, the burden of proof was on the respondent to show that the child had in fact been significantly traumatized or injured.

Table 1 shows that intrusion was the most common form of sexual exploitation; "other and unspecified" acts represent the smallest component of the total. The severity distributions are somewhat surprising. Thus, although no evidence of actual injury was required in the first two categories (i.e., in-scope acts were sufficient to justify a probable injury classification), demonstrable injury was not at all uncommon; proportionately, there were more serious injuries associated with sexual exploitations than with physical assault. Emotional abuse includes three diverse subcategories:

- Verbal or emotional assault: habitual patterns of scape goating, belittling, denigrating or other overly hostile, rejecting treatment, including threats of physical or sexual assault;
- Close confinement: tortuous restrictions of movement, as by tying a

child's arms or legs together, binding a child to a chair or bed, or confining a child to a closet or similar enclosure for prolonged periods; and

- Other/unspecified abusive treatment, which could include attempted physical or sexual assault (e.g., throwing something at a child, but missing), "overworking" or economic exploitation, withholding of food, sleep, or shelter as a form of punishment, or similar purposive acts not encompassed elsewhere.

As shown in Table 1, these "other" problems were by no means uncommon; they constitute about one-third of all in-scope educational neglect problems.

Emotional neglect included three subcategories:

- Inadequate nurturance (extreme parent/guardian inattention to a child's needs for affection, attention, or emotional support) causing or materially contributing to the occurrence or unreasonable prolongation of a serious physical, mental or emotional problem, including but not limited to nonorganic failure-to-thrive;
- Encouragement or permitting of seriously maladaptive behavior (such as severe assaultiveness, chronic delinquency or debilitating drug/alcohol abuse) under circumstances where the parent/guardian had cause to be aware of the existence and seriousness of the problem (e.g., the child had been picked up by the police on previous occasions) and had not attempted to correct it; and
- "Other," which included refusal to permit recommended treatment for a child's diagnosed emotional condition, failure to seek professional assistance for a severely debilitating emotional condition, and extreme overprotectiveness (if implicated in the causation of prolongation of a severely debilitating emotional condition).

As shown in Table 1, inadequate nurturance was the most common form of emotional neglect. No fatalities were attributed to emotional neglect, but of the six major categories of maltreatment, this one had the highest proportion (74 percent) of demonstrably serious injuries/impairments, such as attempted suicides, severe failure-to-thrive, and drug overdoses.

Table 1 shows the severity distribution for each form of maltreatment. In Table 2, the relationship is presented in the other direction, showing the form of maltreatment distribution for each severity category. Fatalities were very uncommon in all major categories, never exceeding 0.34 percent of in-scope children (from Table 1). Table 2 shows that the fatalities which did occur were clustered in two categories, physical assault (72 percent of fatalities) and physical neglect (28 percent). Serious

Table 1
Estimated Number of Recognized In-Scope Children
and Severity Percentage Distribution
by Major Form and Subcategory of Maltreatment

Form and subcategory of maltreatment[1]	No. in-scope children	Severity of child's injury/impairment[2]				
		Fatal[3]	Serious	Moderate	Probable	Total
All forms, total	652,000	0.16	20	63	16	100
Abuse, total	351,100	0.20	12	69	19	100
Physical assault	207,600	0.34	9	78	12	100
Assault with implement/ foreign substance	79,400	0.30	8	76	16	100
Other and unspecified	131,500	0.33	6	78	15	100
Sexual exploitation	44,700	0.02	15	30	54	100
Intrusion	21,400	0	16	17	67	100
Molestation with genital contact	16,000	0	6	16	78	100
Other and unspecified	8,400	0	7	43	50	100
Emotional abuse	138,400	0	16	66	17	100
Verbal/emotional assault	120,200	0	15	63	22	100
Close confinement	3,300	0	4	23	73	100
Other (e.g., threatened or attempted physical or sexual assault)	19,100	0	2	90	8	100
Neglect, total	329,000	0.08	32	55	13	100
Physical neglect	108,000	0.25	46	35	19	100
Abandonment	6,700	0	1	7	91	100
Other refusal of custody	18,900	0	4	31	65	100
Refusal to allow/provide care for diagnosed health condition	40,600	0	25	75	0	100
Failure to seek medical care for serious health condition	16,300	1.06	86	0	12	100
Inadequate physical supervision	6,800	1.22	86	0	13	100
Disregard of avoidable hazards in home	2,800	0.43	99	0	0	100
Inadequate nutrition, clothing, hygiene	17,800	0	85	0	15	100
Other	3,400	0	85	0	16	100
Educational neglect	181,500	0	14	77	9	100
"Permitted" chronic truancy	120,300	0	8	88	4	100
Other (e.g., kept child home, refused to enroll)	61,400	0	19	72	18	100

injuries/impairments were most often associated with physical and emotional neglect.

For the kinds of maltreatment problems encompassed by the research,

Table 1 (Continued)

Form and subcategory of maltreatment[1]	No. in-scope children	Severity of child's injury/impairment[2]				
		Fatal[3]	Serious	Moderate	Probable	Total
Emotional neglect	59,400	0	74	12	10	100
Inadequate nurturance (e.g., failure-to-thrive)	26,000	0	85	0	12	100
"Permitted" chronic maladaptive behavior	14,000	0	93	0	5	100
Other	20,000	0	47	30	17	100

[1]More than one subcategory may apply to an individual child.
[2]The severity measure for maltreatment subcategories is the most serious injury/impairment resulting from acts/omissions in the particular subcategory. Severity measure for major categories is the most serious injury/impairment resulting from all in-scope maltreatment events during the study period.
[3]Percentages expressed to two decimals.

Table 2
Severity of Maltreatment Related Injury or Impairment
by Form of Maltreatment and Age of Child:
Estimated Percentage Distributions by Severity Category

Form of maltreatment and age of child	Severity of injury of impairment				
	Fatal	Serious	Moderate	Probable	Total
Estimated no. of children	1,000	137,400	411,600	102,000	652,000
Form of maltreatment					
Physical assault	72	14	40	24	32
Sexual exploitation	1	5	3	24	7
Emotional abuse	0	16	22	24	21
Physical neglect	28	36	9	20	17
Educational neglect	0	19	34	15	28
Emotional neglect	0	34	1	6	9
Total	101	124	113	113	114
Age of child					
0–2	49	16	5	10	8
3–5	25	7	9	13	9
6–8	2	17	18	15	17
9–11	0	19	18	20	19
12–14	1	14	23	20	21
15–17	23	27	27	22	26
Total	100	100	100	100	100

the Study findings provide the most comprehensive information presently available about the characteristics of maltreated children and their families. Some of the main findings were:

a. Severity

- Eighty-four percent of the "in-scope" children represented in the study evidenced known symptoms of physical or other injuries or impairments as a result of abuse and/or neglect; the remaining 16 percent has experienced forms of maltreatment for which evidence of injury was not required (e.g., sexual exploitation, abandonment) or were assessed, based on circumstantial evidence, as "probably" having experienced demonstrable injury or impairment.
- The proportion of children who experienced serious injuries or impairments as a result of maltreatment was lowest in the area of physical abuse (9 percent), was highest in the area of emotional neglect (74 percent), and was 20 percent overall.
- Deaths resulting from maltreatment were uncommon, constituting less than one percent of the cases (an estimated 1,000 children per year).
- Nearly all maltreatment-caused fatalities resulted from physical assault (72 percent) or physical neglect (28 percent), and most (74 percent) occurred to children under 6 years of age.

b. Age and Sex of Child

- For most forms of maltreatment, incidence rates increased as the age of the child increased.
- In the area of sexual abuse, the age-incidence relationship was not as strong as one might expect: among male victims, incidence rates were essentially constant across age groups, and 50 percent of female sexual abuse victims were 11 years of age or younger.
- At the lower end of the age range, incidence rates from all forms of maltreatment were essentially the same for boys as for girls.
- In the older age groups, abuse incidence rates were substantially higher for girls than for boys, while neglect incidence rates were higher for boys than for girls.

c. Family Income and Ethnicity

- In the higher income groups, incidence rates for all forms of maltreatment were essentially the same for White and Nonwhite children.
- For White children, incidence rates were much higher in the low

income groups than in the higher income groups, for all forms of maltreatment.

- For Nonwhite children, a similarly strong association between poverty and incidence of maltreatment was found, but only in the neglect area; abuse incidence rates were essentially constant (at low level) across income levels for Nonwhite children.

d. Type of County

- Overall incidence rates were somewhat lower in suburban counties than in urban or rural counties.
- Sexual abuse was proportionately more common in rural counties than elsewhere.
- Educational neglect was proportionately more common in urban counties than elsewhere.
- Emotional abuse and emotional neglect were proportionately somewhat more common in suburban counties than elsewhere.

e. Other Variables

- Incidence rates were somewhat higher in families with a single child or with four or more children than families with two to three children.
- The only form of maltreatment where a substantial proportion of the involved adults were persons other than biological parents was sexual abuse. In that area, father substitutes (primarily stepfathers) were involved in 34 percent of the cases and non-parental perpetrators were involved in 32 percent of the cases. Even in this area, however, biological mothers were involved—at least to the extent of having known about the problem and having allowed it to continue—in a significant fraction of the cases (43 percent).

Public schools are reporting about 100,000 cases per year to agencies. However, nearly half of these reports are not substantiated, frequently because the reported problem is-inappropriate or not serious enough. Yet, public schools identified to this study nearly seven times more in-scope cases than they reported. Most of these cases, presumably, were serious enough to be reported.

These findings (together with similar findings for other agencies) suggest that, although much has been accomplished in heightening public awareness of the general problem of child abuse and neglect, much remains to be done to educate the public (and particularly the major professional groups in the community) about the specific circumstances and situations for which reporting is or is not appropriate. It appears that reporting of inappropriate cases (resulting in a wasteful expenditure of resources in investigation and processing of cases which ultimately receive no services) and nonreporting of appropriate cases (resulting in a lack of needed services) are both occurring on a large scale and that both are major problems in the current child protection system.

In the area of emotional abuse, incidence rates increase gradually with increasing age for both sexes. There is no appreciable sex difference in incidence until the 15–17 age groups, at which point the incidence rate for girls suddenly jumps to almost three times the rate for boys. It is intriguing that such a pronounced increase occurs in the 15–17 group and that it occurs only for girls. The reasons for the increase, however, are not readily apparent.

Physical neglect is the only form of maltreatment for which the incidence curve has a generally downward slope for both boys and girls. For both sexes, the age group at greatest risk is 0–2. No doubt, this curve reflects the extreme physical dependence of infants and the decline in physical dependence with occurs as children get older.

Since educational neglect involves school-related problems, it is essentially nonexistent until age 6. Then and thereafter, the incidence rate is higher for boys than for girls. For boys, incidence rates increase sharply and evenly over the 6–17 age range. One might speculate that, in families where educational neglect occurs at all, the problem tends to be chronic and cumulative in its manifestations. Such an interpretation may work for boys, but doesn't seem to apply to girls. For girls, the jagged age curve is not suggestive of long term cumulative problems.

Finally, the incidence of serious emotional neglect is substantially higher for boys than for girls from age six onward. For both sexes, the incidence rates are constant from age 6–14 and then increase significantly during the years 15–17.

Relationships between child's ethnic group and major form of maltreatment are presented in the bottom portion of Table 3. Compared to their representation in the national population (15 percent), Black children are underrepresented in all abuse categories and in all neglect categories except educational neglect. Educational neglect is a large category, however, and the overrepresentation of Blacks is substantial (27 percent of children in-scope for educational neglect vs. the 15 percent of U.S. Children). Because of this, the overall representation of Blacks among in-scope children is about the same as in the general population (16 percent).

White children constitute 83 percent of the child population. It may be seen that this group is proportionately overrepresented in all maltreatment categories except educational neglect.

An estimated 55 percent of all U. S. children live in families with annual income of $15,000 or more, and only 17 percent live in families with incomes under $7,000. In comparison to the income distribution for all U.S. children, children from low income families are overrepresented in all maltreatment categories. Not to the same extent, however: the strongest relationships between poverty and maltreatment occur in the areas of physical and educational neglect, where over half of all in-scope children were reported to live in families with income under $7,000. Overall, the relationship is substantially less pronounced for abuse than neglect: 34 percent of all in-scope abused children have family incomes under $7,000, as compared to 53 percent of in-scope neglected children. The forms of maltreatment recognized proportionately more often in families of $15,000 or more than in lower income families are emotional neglect and emotional abuse.

Age by sex relationships for the major forms of in-scope abuse and neglect are presented in Table 3. In the 0–2 age group, there are essentially no sex differences in incidence. In that age group, incidence rates for boys are nearly identical to those for girls, for all forms of maltreatment. Second, there is a consistent pattern of sex differences increasing with increasing age, the largest sex differences occurred in the 15–17 group. Third, the direction of the sex difference in the upper age range is different for abuse than for neglect. For all three forms of abuse, incidence rates are substantially higher for girls than for boys in the upper age range, and the reverse is true for two of the three major neglect categories; the one exception is physical neglect, where incidence rates are slightly higher for girls than for boys in the 12–17 are range.

Among girls, the incidence of physical abuse gradually increases with increasing age. For boys, 3–5 seems to be the peak age, and incidence rates gradually decline thereafter. It is curious that the incidence rate is so much higher for boys than girls in the 3–5 age group, but nowhere else along the age spectrum. It is also interesting that the measured incidence of physical abuse of boys declines during the teenage years: one wonders whether physical abuse of boys occurs less often then, or is just less often recognized.

Table 3
Form of Maltreatment by Child Demographic Characteristics:
Percent of Estimated Total Number of In-Scope Maltreated Children

| | Form of maltreatment | | | | | | | | |
| | Abuse | | | | Neglect | | | | |
Child characteristics	Physi-cal	Sexual	Emo-tional	Total	Physi-cal	Educa-tional	Emo-tional	Total	Total
Estimated no.									
children (1,000)	207.6	44.7	138.4	351.1	108.0	181.5	59.4	329.1	652.0
Age of child									
(% known)	(99)	(99)	(99)	(100)	(99)	(99)	(100)	(99)	(99)
0–2	11	2	3	7	23	0	6	9	8
3–5	17	6	9	12	9	3	5	5	9
6–8	17	11	17	17	20	18	13	18	17
9–11	16	21	19	18	18	19	16	18	19
12–14	19	28	20	21	14	29	20	22	21
15–17	20	32	32	25	16	31	40	28	26
Total	100	100	100	100	100	100	100	100	100
Sex of child									
(% known)	(99)	(99)	(100)	(99)	(100)	(99)	(100)	(100)	(100)
Boys	47	17	43	43	53	63	72	61	52
Girls	53	83	57	57	47	37	28	39	48
Total	100	100	100	100	100	100	100	100	100
Child's ethnic group[1]									
(% known)	(99)	(99)	(99)	(99)	(99)	(99)	(99)	(99)	(99)
White	86	88	92	89	84	72	89	77	82
Black	13	11	7	10	15	27	11	22	16
Other	1	1	1	1	2	1	1	1	1
Total	100	100	100	100	100	100	100	100	100

[1]For comparison with Census data, "White" includes "White, not of Hispanic origin" and "Hispanic."

Elderly Abuse*

Although there are no national incidence data available, elder abuse appears to be a serious, and perhaps widespread, problem. Estimates of the extent of elder abuse vary from 500,000 to 1,000,000 victims annually. The House Committee on Aging estimates that only one in six cases is actually reported.

---

*Reprinted from RESPONSE to the Victimization of Women and Children Center for Women Policy Studies

Three factors limit access to accurate information about elder abuse: unclear and differing definitions used by researchers, lack of awareness of the problem, and reluctance by victims to report or admit abuse for fear of retaliation in the form of further abuse, abandonment, or institutionalization. When victims do complain of abuse, their reports are sometimes dismissed as symptoms of paranoia or senility.

Although definitions of elder abuse vary, four classifications of abuse are commonly used:

Physical Abuse — conduct that results in bodily harm;

Psychological Abuse — threats or actions that result in mental distress, fright, and emotional disturbance;

Negligence — breach of duty or careless conduct that results in injury or in a violation of her rights; and

Financial Exploitation — theft or conversion of money or property belonging to the older person.

Three of four major contemporary studies of elder abuse found a significant level of physical and psychological abuse within their sample. The most common forms are the result of neglect that results in physical and emotional injury. Frequently more than one type of abuse is present.

In the Massachusetts study, physical trauma constituted over 41 percent of the injuries (bruises, welts, cuts, punctures, fractures, dislocations, and burnings). Verbal harassment, malnutrition, financial mismanagement, unreasonable confinement, oversedation, and sexual abuse were also reported.

In the Michigan study, passive neglect, followed by verbal and emotional abuse were found to be the most prevalent forms. Active neglect (the deliberate withholding of necessary items or assistance) and physical abuse were found to exist to a far lower degree.

In the Ohio study, physical abuse occurred most frequently, in nearly 75 percent of all cases; direct beatings occurred in 28 percent of the cases, and psychological abuse, in 51 percent.

In the Maryland study, psychological abuse was found most frequently; direct beatings were cited in 15 percent of the cases.

Elder abuse, like other forms of family violence, is rarely an isolated occurrence; it usually recurs, sometimes frequently and over an extended period. Because of the frailty of its victims, elder abuse is always serious and sometimes fatal. Elder abuse is found among families of all socioeconomic levels.

Abusers are usually related to the victim and live in the same household. Often the abuser is the victim's primary caregiver. The Massachusetts study revealed that 86 percent of the abusers were relatives: 24 percent were sons, 20 percent husbands, and 15 percent daughters. The Maryland study showed that 81 percent of abusers were relatives: 42 percent were their children; 50 percent were female; most were white (88 percent), middle class (65 percent), and middle-aged (53 percent). In the Ohio study, 90 percent of the abusers were relatives; the highest number were daughters followed by sons, granddaughters, husbands, and siblings.

The Detroit study revealed a correlation between the gender of the abuser and the type of abuse. Sons were more likely to engage in active, direct abuse. They were responsible for two-thirds of the physical abuse and nearly 30 percent of the emotional abuse. Daughters were most likely to be involved in emotional neglect.

Victims are usually female, over age 75, and with some physical or mental impairment (often a combination) which prevents them from handling all of the tasks of daily living (dressing, preparing meals, toileting, etc.):

In the Massachusetts study, 80 percent of the victims were female, 36 percent were over the age of 80, and 75 percent had a physical or mental disability.

In the Maryland study, 81 percent of the victims were female, and their mean age was 84; 96 percent suffered from some form of physical disability and over half from a moderate to severe mental impairment.

In the Ohio study, 77 percent of the victims were female, 75 percent were severely impaired, 58 percent were widowed, and 75 percent white.

In the Detroit study, 75 percent of the victims were female, 40 percent were black, and 56 percent white; although religion as not always known, 35 percent of the sample were Protestant, 17 percent Catholic, and there was only one Jewish victim. Most victims in the Detroit study were fairly isolated. Although most had at least one non-household family contact, this contact mainly consisted of a visit or phone call every week or less. Nearly three-quarters of the victims had no friend outside the family with whom they had contact.

Several causal theories of elder abuse have been posited. It is likely that several of these (and perhaps other factors) interact to produce an abusive situation:

Several impairments common among the very old lead to dependence upon family members who may not be emotionally, financially, or otherwise able to meet the stringent demands of long-term caregiving. Frustration, resentment, exhaustion, and/or guilt build to the point where it is released in the form of abusive behavior.

Situational stress factors such as poverty, isolation, or lack of support from other family members cause people to abuse family members.

Personality traits of abusers or character disorders cause them to be abusive. Some abusers are mentally ill, retarded, or alchoholic and unable to make appropriate judgments and provide adequate care.

Violence is a learned behavior and children who abuse their parents were likely to have been abused by them as children.

Widely held negative attitudes and stereotypes about older persons that devalue and dehumanize them in the eyes of others, make them more vulnerable to maltreatment.

To date, there is no federal legislation that addresses the problem of elder abuse. About half of the states have some protective services legislation although many states do not allocate funds to counties to support programs to protect abused adults.

Over twenty states have mandatory elder abuse reporting laws. These vary significantly and are difficult to enforce. In Connecticut, for example, everyone is required to report; in New Hampshire, only physicians. Within three years after Connecticut's law went into effect 3,380 cases of elder abuse were reported.

When elder abuse is reported, legal and service options are limited. Often, victims are placed in nursing homes for lack of better alternatives. Congregate living facilities may be appropriate for some victims but are not always available. Most board and care homes do not accept residents who cannot care for themselves; many are unlicensed and substandard. Some victims choose to stay in abusive situations because their alternatives seem worse.

Services that have been found to be successful in helping family caregivers cope with the stress of caring for elders include respite care, geriatric day care, in-home supportive services, self-help groups for caregivers, congregate and home-delivered meals, and social activities for elders provided in senior centers and other community locations.

Conclusion

Violence perpetrated by family members on each other is widespread and growing.

Familar patterns of wife abuse develop in three phases—the tension building phase, the explosion and the loving phase—and will usually recur unless there is therapeutic intervention.

The genesis of child abuse is in a child rearing style characterized by pervasive, premature demands on children, who are stoutly punished when they fail to produce, and who themselves often grow up to be abusers.

Annually, between 500,000 and one million elderly people, primarily women, are physically and psychologically abused, neglected and financially exploited. Many of these older Americans have physical or mental impairments which force them to reside with family members, who abuse and exploit them.

BIBLIOGRAPHY

Center for Women Policy Studies. *Child Abuse: The Facts.* Washington, D.C.: Center, 1985.

Center for Women Policy Studies. *Elder Abuse: The Facts.* Washington, D.C.: Center, 1985.

Center for Women Policy Studies. *Wife Abuse: The Facts.* Vol. 7, Number 1, Washington, D.C.: Center, 1983.

Dobash, R. E. and Dobash, R. P. *Violence Against Wives.* New York: Free Press, 1979

Jaffe, Natalie. *Assaults on Women.* New York: Public Affairs Committee, Inc., 1981.

National Institute of Mental Health. *Plain Talk About Wife Abuse.* Rockville, MD, 1983.

Straus, Murray A. "Wife Beating: How Common and Why." *Victimology,* Vol. 2, 1978.

U. S. Department of Health and Human Services. *National Study of the Incidence and Severity of Child Abuse and Neglect.* Washington, D.C.: U. S. Dept. H.H.S., 1981.

Walker, Lenoire. *The Battered Woman.* New York: Harper & Row, 1979

Chapter 4

HOUSEHOLD BURGLARY

Two teenagers, who had been watching a house in their neighborhood for weeks, until the occupants left on vacation, force a sliding glass door from its frame with a crow bar, then proceed to systematically vandalize the home before leaving with a small black and white portable television set valued at 95 dollars. A lone young man quietly pries open the rear bedroom window of a luxury home, only be thwarted in his attempt at theft by the siren from a burglar alarm that causes him to flee empty-handed. After ringing the door bell to a second floor apartment in a middle-class neighborhood, a magazine salesman spontaneously tries the front door, finds it unlocked, enters the unoccupied apartment, steals a camera and some jewelry, then leaves the way he came in.

The preceeding cases are all burglaries, and each represents one of the three recognized categories of household burglary: *forcible entry*, in which a structure is entered by intruders through force, such as smashing a window or jimmying a door; *attempted forcible entry*, in which a forcible entry is tried but interrupted before fulfillment; and *unlawful entry without force*, in which an intruder gains entry through an open or unlocked door or window, or by use of a stolen key. The distinction between types of burglary—whether forced, attempted or unforced—is an important one in trying to understand the nature and extent of residential burglary in America.

A Profile of Burglary in America

If you have not been victimized by a burglary, you may be in a shrinking minority. There are approximately 85 million households in America. A ten year study by the federal government, revealed that 73 million of them had been burglarized, resulting in billions of dollars in losses.* More than two out of three burglaries across the country involved residential structures—primarily owned houses and rental apartments—not businesses. About forty-five percent of these crimes entailed unlawful entry without force, one-third were actual forceable entries and less than one-quarter were unsuccessful attempts.

There are important seasonal fluctuations to burglary, which occurs most often in the warm summer months and peaks in July and August. There are various explanations for this, including the greater tendency of people to leave doors and windows open during the summertime and the fact that householders seem more inclined to be outside away from home, even on vacation, from June to September. While winter is not burglary-free, it is the season of least occurrence, with February the lowest month.

It is impossible to pinpoint with any degree of accuracy exactly what time of day burglaries tend to take place since they occur most often when people are away for extended periods. But, in those incidents in which a time was known, over thirty-five percent took place between the hours of six a.m. and six p.m., making burglary primarily a daytime crime. Burglaries that take place during the nighttime hours are more likely to be unsuccessful attempts than those which occurred in daylight.

A renter is more likely to be burglarized than a home owner. Householders who reside in single family houses have significantly lower victimization rates than those who occupy homes in multi-unit dwellings. The most vulnerable apartment premises are those made up of from five to nine units, too small to have sophisticated security but large enough to be impersonal. Larger buildings, of say, twenty-five or more units, are probably more secure because of the greater vehicular and pedestrian traffic, which increases the perception personal surveillance. Urban households, whether rental or owned homes, have the highest burglary rates; rural areas the lowest.

Unlawful Entry Without Force

In a society which seems to be as concerned about crime as this one, it is startling that so many burglaries result because of unsecured premises. No force entries are the largest single category of household burglaries,

---

*The figure may be slightly misleading since some of the burglarized homes were victimized more than once.

representing forty-five percent of all such crimes, with an average annual loss of some 400 million dollars.

At lease one-third of all entrys without force were gained *indirectly*, through garages or other non-dwelling areas. The primary entry points were, of course, opened or unlocked windows or doors, or doors which were unlocked by a key assailants found "hidden" on the premises.

In any given year, there will be some three million or so unforced burglaries, or around 8,000 per day. The U. S. Justice Department, which has studied household burglary in depth, became so perplexed and exasperated by this phenomenon that it asserted:

> Although victim responsibility might be to some observers too harsh a term, it is clear that many households are guilty of negligence and some are more negligent than others; for example, the family that leaves home with the garage door open or a housekey placed invitingly under a doormat is assuredly more careless than the family that closed but failed to lock a second-story window. Ultimately, the degree of negligence rests, at least in part, on the nature of the *cues* the victim leaves and the extent to which these cues prompt or motivate criminal activity. When the cue proves to be a major motivating force, that is to say when an individual who would not otherwise have acted seized upon a perceived opportunity and commits a burglary, the victims must certainly *share the blame*.

Burglary is by and large a crime of opportunity. In non-forced entry, Americans by the millions are furnishing criminals with opportunities of epic proportions, and burglars are making good their advantage, as indicated by the fact that fully 80 percent of all losses from this form of burglary are neither recovered nor recouped through insurance. It cannot be stated too strongly that unlawful entry without force is by any definition a preventable crime.

Who Are Those Burglars

Who can forget the sight of Cary Grant, fashionably clad entirely in black, a silk scarf worn rakishly around his neck, stealthily gliding along the roof tiles of a French country home, on the trail of a rival jewel thief whose victims have included spoiled dowagers, captains of industry and royalty. The burglar depicted in Hitchcocks "To Catch a Thief" was heroic, larger than life, exciting, even enviable. Burglars have been romanticized in fiction as crafty, courageous individualists who stole from those who could afford it, and who used the proceeds of their profession to live with style and flair. Notable movie burglars have ranged from Errol Flynn to Ryan O'Neal, David Niven to James Caan. These movie thieves were fascinating characters who led the good life, and whose portrayals bore a less than flirting relationship with reality.

Very few burglars are Cary Grant. Almost all of them are male, but that is the closest resemblance they bear to their glamorous movie counterparts. Three-quarters of all arrested burglars are under thirty years of age. In any given year, a significant number of arrestees are under twenty. Fully one-quarter are juveniles who often cause more damage to a burglarized property than the value of goods they steal.

If one were to profile a "typical" burglar, it would be a poor young man from an unstable single parent home who, along with one associate of similar background, breaks into a residence close to his own home and takes a modest amount of property. He will not be a specialist, but an opportunist who steals in the easiest way available from the least challenging targets. A substantial number of assailants will be under the influence of drugs or alcohol during entry. In surveys of incarcerated burglars, about fifty percent were drunk or drugged at the time of their crimes.

There is, however, another type of thief: the professional burglar. These career criminals are significantly older than burglars in general, and have acquired skills which permit them to select more lucrative targets and painstakingly plan their attack. They may have learned to pick locks, defeat alarms, choose weak entry points and plot exit routes. Some are even so-called "cat burglars" who either scale building elevations, or surreptitiously enter "secure" condominiums or slip into dwellings while occupants sleep, eat, or watch television. A growing number of these burglars now employ robbery as well as unlawful entry, as they hold up homeowners at gunpoint. These professionals only steal what they can spend (cash) or readily sell to a fence, with whom most have a business relationship. There are very few truly professional burglars; they probably number considerably less than five percent of the offender group. Since they victimize an affluent clientele, the risk of capture is great because the security devices and precautions they must overcome are generally quite extensive.

Surveys of inmate populations reveal the hazards of burglary. Fully one in five of all inmates in jails and prisons were convicted of burglary. Most had been to prison before and are destined to return again.

In an earlier time, burglary was viewed by scholars as a crime by strangers in which someone unknown to the victim would break in and steal property. Some of the most recent studies of household burglary have cast doubt on that notion by pointing out that a substantial minority of these crimes are committed by people known by the victim. In about one out of ten residential burglaries the assailant is captured and identified and there is enough information available to determine the relationship of the victim to the offender, if any. Approximately thirty-five percent of those crimes involved assailants who knew their victims personally, including twenty-five percent by acquaintances, four percent by relatives and approximately eight percent by former spouses. This seemingly high percentage of "acquaintance burglary" may also be do to the fact that these types of assailants are caught and identified more readily than strangers.

Burglary does not seem to be a crime in which offenders specialize. The "rap sheets" of convicted burglars indicate that most have had a rich and diverse history of criminal involvement. Many have been arrested for violent crimes as well as property offenses, sometimes dating back to their early teen years. The older a man gets, the greater the likelihood that he will eventually specialize if he becomes a career criminal.

The Tools of Burglary

The idea that a burglar carries with him an array of tools neatly fitted into a satchel is true in a slim number of instances. Certainly in the case of commercial safecrackers, a dying breed of American outlaw, this may be so, as well as in some of the more complex commercial break-ins. The devices used may be bulky, sophisticated and specifically adapted for the work. Yet these are exceptions to the rule; i.e.—burglars are not generally well-equipped criminals.

Some burglars carry no tools whatsoever. They will simply look for an easy mark and either enter an unsecured door or window, or they will use tools that are available on the property they intend to victimize. Burglars who do carry some tools usually stick to the basics: screwdriver; crow bar; all purpose knife; flashlight. It is becoming increasingly rare for assailants to carry with them tools that have been adapted for the purpose of breaking in homes. Most states have passed laws which make "burglars' tools"—those which have been modified for criminal purposes—illegal in and of themselves. People who carry these devices can be arrested just for having them in their possession. So, regular hardware tools that can be carried unobtrusively are usually preferred, with heavy duty screwdrivers topping the list of favorites, valuable information for a woman who wants to secure her home properly.

What They Take

Opportunistic juvenile burglars and high level professional thieves have one thing in common: neither generally ransacks a house and makes off with all or most of its contents. Naturally there are some cases in which a woman may return home to her apartment to find every stick of furniture gone, but this is a very rare occurrence.

Thieves prefer to steal small, valuable items that can be easily disposed of. When furniture, appliances and equipment are stolen, selected items are usually taken, items which can either be carried away by hand or can be transported to a nearby getaway vehicle or can be driven off in the victim's own car stolen from the premises. It is not at all unusual to find that articles left behind by burglars are considerably more valuable — and of greater weight and bulk—than the ones they take.

In a study of unlawful entries into apartments and single family houses, it was found that burglars made off with a wide variety of property, but there were some favorites. The items taken, in order of preference, were:

Cash

Televisions, stereo equipment, cameras

Bicycles and parts

Jewelry, furs, silverware and precious metals, such as coins

Motor vehicles and parts

Guns and ammunition

Tools and building supplies

Home furnishings

Food and drink

Clothing

Sporting goods

The Potential of Violence

A woman returns home from her job as a registered nurse in the surgical intensive care unit of a moderate-sized private hospital. The moment she enters her ground floor apartment, she senses that something is wrong. She leaves and calls a neighbor, who accompanies her into the unit, where they discover that an intruder has pried open and entered through an awning window in the bathroom and stolen a camera, some inexpensive jewelry and a portable radio. The loss totals approximately 600 dollars, plus thirty-two dollars worth of damage to the window.

This example represents the popular conception of a burglary. Someone breaks in while the occupants are gone, steals property and leaves. Sometimes the loss is recovered; more often it is not. Burglary—a crime against property. But there is a flip side to this coin, one which is becoming increasingly more widespread.

A businesswoman drives to her single family home in a fashionable suburban residential area, after a pleasant dinner with friends. She is divorced and her two preteenage children are spending the week with their father. She pulls into the driveway, gets out, strides down the walkway, and unlocks the front door. Once inside, she goes to her bedroom, undresses and showers, then goes straight to bed, where she falls immediately into a deep sleep. At 2:15 a.m., she is awakened by a noise. She sits up in bed and sees a man standing over her. The intruder, who had forced open a sliding glass door in the rear of the house, tells the woman he has a gun and will kill her if she disobeys his instructions. He binds her, rapes her, takes 75 dollars in cash and a wristwatch, then leaves.

This is the other face of burglary, and it is an ugly one indeed. There is some evidence that women for years have been frightened of burglary because of an intuitive feeling that such crimes were potentially violent ones to households headed by women. Yet, most everyone, from scholars to law enforcement officers, often reassured women by pointing out that burglars were thieves who tried diligently to avoid detection, and thus would flee at the slightest sign of a resident. This reassurance was often patronizing and condescending. In the light of recent research into household burglary, it also turned out to be dangerous advice.

The fear that a burglar may inflict physical injuries or worse on the occupant of a dwelling who just happens to be home during the break-in is a well-founded one. Unhappily, burglaries are becoming increasingly violent. Consider the evidence. Over the last decade, almost three million violent crimes were committed in the course of residential burglaries. During a recent three year period, there were greater than 100,000 burglaries that escalated into robberies, often armed robberies, when the burglar and a resident came into contact with one another. In a study of burglaries in which a resident was home, the federal government found more alarming outcomes. For every 100 burglaries there were five rapes, 38 robberies, 48 auto thefts and 55 felonious assaults. It should be noted that the additional offenses were so numerous because there were often multiple crimes (e.g. rape and robbery) during a single burglary. Nevertheless, this data is very distressing and there is even more bad news associated with the phenomenon.

Violence in the commission of a burglary usually occurs when an occupant either happens to be at home during the crime or is unfortunate enough to stumble on it in-progress. Yet, there seems to be a growing trend among criminals to burglarize homes which they *know* are occupied, a real break with the traditional dogma on burglary. Rape, robbery and auto theft, then, are not merely opportunistic dividends for burglars, they have become planned outcomes.

Burglary can no longer be neatly classified as a property crime. The risk of injury to householders is so great in residential burglaries that it is perilously misleading to suggest that assaultive behavior is just the spontaneous action of a thief surprised in the act. Violence is often a foreseeable and intended consequence of household burglary. That is the bad news. The good news is that most household burglaries are preventable crimes that can be deterred through the application of security devices and sensible precautions designed to reduce opportunities and dissuade even highly motivated burglars. In any event, the crime deserves special attention from women, considering the cost and potential dangers involved.

Conclusion

We know a great deal about household burglaries. More than 85 percent of all American households have been burglarized during the last decade. Burglary is a seasonal crime with most occurring in the warm summer months; winter is the season of least frequency. A high percentage of break-ins take place in the daylight hours. Most burglars do not know their victims, but a substantial minority are acquaintances, relatives or ex-spouses.

Over the past ten years, almost 30 million households gave burglars unrestricted access to their homes by failing to lock doors, or by leaving windows open or by hiding a key in places which were so obvious that it was found and used to gain unlawful entry. These so-called unforced entries represent the most numerous category of burglary.

Rather few burglars are sleek professionals; most are ill-equipped young men who hit targets of opportunity. They rarely "clean out" a home, preferring to take selected items such as cash, electronics gear, bicycles, jewelry, furs silverware and precious metals.

The most disturbing aspect of burglary is its potentially violent nature. A great many people are assaulted in their homes because they were unfortunate enough to be there during a break-in, or because a burglar purposely targeted them for rape or robbery.

The irony of burglary is that it is largely a preventable crime which continues to victimize people because of what the U. S. Justice Department calls "household negligence," a form a carelessness which is more an act of omission than one of commission.

BIBLIOGRAPHY

Bureau of Justice Statistics, "Household Burglary" in *Bureau of Justice Statistics Bulletin.* Washington: U. S. Department of Justice, 1985.

_____, "The Severity of Crime," 1984.

_____, "The Victims of Crime," 1981.

Bureau of Justice Statistics, *Report to the Nation on Crime and Justice.* Washington: U. S. Government Printing Office, 1983.

Macdonald, John M., C. Ronald Brannan and Robert E. Nicoletti, *Burglary and Theft.* Springfield, Ill.: Charles C Thomas, Publisher, 1980.

National Criminal Justice Information and Statistics Service, *The Cost of Negligence: Losses from Preventable Household Burglaries.* Washington: U. S. Department of Justice, 1979.

Shenk, J. Frederick and Patsy A. Klaus, "The Economic Cost of Crime to Victims" in *Bureau of Justice Statistics Special Report.* Washington: U. S. Department of Justice, 1984.

Chapter 5

CRIME, SECURITY AND THE NEIGHBORHOOD

Crime in residential communities is a major American concern. In this chapter, two related issues are addressed: 1. physical characteristics and informal territorial control in high and low crime neighborhoods; and 2. neighborhood organizations and informal citizen action and crime prevention.

Environment, Territoriality and Neighborhood Crime*

Abundant literature exists on the relationship between neighborhood physical and social conditions and crime. However, there are several major problems with this body of research. One is that studies showing a relationship between poverty and crime take a monolithic view of low income neighborhoods. They do not explain why some poor neighborhoods are relatively safe, while others are dangerous. Second, studies tend to examine either social conditions or physical design, rather than taking both into account. Third, while many studies infer that the effect of social or physical characteristics on crime is transmitted through informal social control, this latter factor is seldom actually measured.

This section focuses on both objective characteristics of neighborhoods that have been linked to crime and the informal territorial control in neighborhoods that is believed to transmit the effects of objective conditions. The literature on the relationship between the objective conditions and crime will be reviewed first. Objective conditions are defined as physical design, social characteristics, and characteristics of neighborhood boundaries. Informal territorial control and its relation to crime will be discussed later.

Three general categories of physical characteristics have been associated with neighborhood crime: building type, land use, and the street design.

---

*Reprinted with editorial adaption from Greenberg, Rohe & Williams. *Safe and Secure Neighborhoods.* Wash, D.C.: U. S. Department of Justice, 1982.

The underlying theme of this research is that physical design can either foster or retard social interaction among neighbors, informal street surveillance, and a proprietary attitude toward the neighborhood. All of these are believed to deter crime.

Oscar Newman's (1972) study of the effect on crime of physical design, particularly buildings and streets spawned a large number of subsequent studies on the notion of defensible space. Newman found in a study of public housing that the taller the building, the higher the crime rate. He also reported that residents of high-rise public housing displayed greater animosity toward police than those in low-rise projects. He inferred from these findings that in tall buildings there is a forced disassociation between dwellings and street activities and a sense of alienation both from the surrounding neighborhood and other residents of the project. Thus, areas with a high proportion of high-rise dwellings would be expected to have higher crime rates than those characterized by low-rise structures.

Related to the issue of height, it has also been found that neighborhoods with a high proportion of single-family dwellings have lower crime rates than those dominated by multi-family dwellings. The explanation offered for this finding is that residence in a single-family dwelling encourages more of a proprietary attitude toward the surrounding area than residence in a multi-family building.

Proponents of the defensible space perspective assert that the more the street design is able to delineate public and private areas, the greater its effectiveness in reducing crime. A street that accommodates large numbers of people living outside the neighborhood increases both the number of potential victims and offenders in the neighborhood. In addition, the large number of people who use these streets makes it difficult for residents of the area to distinguish neighbors from strangers, and therefore weakens the neighborhood's informal surveillance capacity. Studies have found that the location of major arteries in residential areas increases residential burglary and fear of crime. Thus, low crime neighborhoods are expected to have fewer major streets than adjacent high crime neighborhoods.

Several other aspects of street design are also believed to affect crime. Building setbacks, street lighting, and visual obstructions created by shrubbery, high fences, and the like all directly affect the ability of neighborhood residents to informally surveil the area. Surveillance is more difficult in blocks with severely staggered building setbacks than in blocks with straight line setbacks. The findings on the effect of street lighting on crime are mixed. A study by Wright found that the intensity of lighting had a negative effect on violent crime like assault and robbery but little effect on property crimes. In contrast, Reppetto's study of residential crime found no systematic relationship for either robbery or burglary.

Jacobs assets that diverse land use is a key element in crime deterrence. By diverse land use, Jacobs means that neighborhoods and blocks within neighborhoods have many different functions, that is residential, commercial, institutional, and leisure. Multi-functional areas will attract a continual flow of people throughout the day and evening hours. Jacobs suggests that this is the most effective means of insuring informal surveillance, what she refers to as "a basic supply of activities and eyes." In contrast, the domination of a single land use, regardless of what it is, results in a scheduling of use, such that the area is guaranteed to be deserted for long periods of time. Despite the persuasiveness of Jacobs' arguments, diversity *per se* may not be sufficient to reduce crime. Dietrick found that residential burglary occurred more frequently near commercial areas. Moreover, certain commercial establishments (liquor stores, bars, adult book stores) and service facilities (methadone clinics) may attract potential offenders to the area and thereby promote crime. Thus, both the extent and type of diversity must be taken into account. In addition, land use that created boundaries may also have an effect on crime. Depending on its location, a railroad, expressway or commercial district may help reduce crime by creating or reinforcing neighborhood boundaries or may help to increase crime by slicing through the core of the neighborhood.

Research on the social correlates of crime has a long history, beginning with the classical ecological studies of Chicago in the 1920's. The bulk of the literature shows that crime is most prevalent in poor, nonwhite, transient areas. The usual explanations are that such areas both breed and attract criminals and lack the cohesion to deter criminals coming from within or outside. However, the major problem with this research is that it usually does not go beyond simple statistical correlations to an understanding of the underlying relationships.

Four neighborhood social characteristics have been emphasized in the literature: economic status, race, residential stability, and life cycle stage of the residents.

Many studies show that crime rates tend to be highest in low income, predominantly black, neighborhoods near the city's core. However, it may not be that a high percentage of blacks or poor people, *per se,* promotes crime but rather that they tend to have low rates of home ownership which may discourage the formation of close ties to and a sense of responsibility for the neighborhood.

Studies have suggested that crime is lower in residentially stable than in unstable neighborhoods. The underlying assumption is that long-term residence results in the formation of strong emotional ties to the neighborhood, the ability to distinguish between neighbors and strangers, and the development of informal interaction with others living in the area. These qualities are often viewed as the best defense against crime. In a study of a poor Chicago neighborhood stable Italian, Mexican, and Puerto Rican communities were able to form "an extensive communication network in which personal information is freely revealed and can travel beyond the range of face-to-face relations." These areas had fewer burglaries and robberies than surrounding areas. Blacks, who lived primarily in a large public housing project, were unable to form what Suttles refers to as a "stable moral community." One major reason for this was the enforced transiency, since it was necessary to move out once the family's income exceeded a certain level.

Poor and black neighborhoods are typically viewed as targets for crime. However, this may be true because these areas also tend to be transient. In attempting to explain differences in crime between neighborhoods, it is therefore important to separate the effects of stability from those of economic and racial composition.

The life cycle stage of individuals is defined by their age and family type. Abundant individual level evidence links crime to adolescence and early adulthood. Neighborhoods with a large proportion of adolescents would therefore be expected to have high crime rates, particularly for crimes which tend to be locally committed. Victimization surveys show high rates of fear of crime among the elderly but low rates of victimization. Thus, neighborhoods with a high percentage of elderly people would be expected to have high fear of crime but low rates of objectively measured crime.

With regard to family types, neighborhoods with a large number of families with young children, that is family oriented neighborhoods, may be well defended against crime. Children and mothers with children have the clearest view of the internal structure of the neighborhood and the greatest stake in its safety, because they spend more time on the street than others. They tend to know more people in the neighborhood and are most involved in information exchange. In contrast, neighborhoods dominated by childless households may not be as well defended, because fewer people are on the street during the day. Thus, holding other variables constant, family oriented neighborhoods should have lower crime than neighborhoods dominated by childless households.

Equally as important as internal characteristics in differentiating between high and low crime neighborhoods may be the characteristics of neighborhood boundaries.

The critical difference in crime levels between two adjacent neighborhoods may be the characteristics of their other borders. A "buffer zone" or "no-man's land" separating two neighborhoods is an area in which no one lives permanently and over which no one exercises control. It is, therefore, regarded as dangerous. Railroads, expressways, and large industrial concentrations are examples of such areas. Because few people venture into them, they may inhibit potentially antagonistic people from entering a neighborhood. Furthermore, anyone who crosses such boundaries is likely to be immediately obvious to neighborhood residents. Thus, a neighborhood with such a "buffer zone" may have less crime than a nearby area without one. Second, a low crime neighborhood may be a transition area between a transient, low income neighborhood and a stable, middle income neighborhood. In this case the low crime neighborhood would be closer to an area that is likely to have lower crime, or at least fewer criminals residing there, than the adjacent but high crime neighborhood. In a related vein is the possible spill-over of crime from nearby areas. Two adjacent and similar neighborhoods may have different crime rates because the high crime neighborhood is surrounded on its other borders by high crime neighborhoods. Crime from nearby areas may, therefore, spill over and increase the level of crime. While there is little empirical evidence on this issue, it is hypothesized that the characteristics of boundaries may be as important as internal characteristics in distinguishing between adjacent high and low crime neighborhoods.

Informal Citizen Action and Crime Prevention*

What is informal social control and how is it different from other types of social control? Why is informal social control important to those interested in crime prevention? What are the conditions necessary for the development of informal social control? These are the questions addressed in this chapter.

In most general terms social control can be defined as the use of rewards or punishments to insure that members of a group—such as a family, organization, neighborhood or society—will obey the group's rules or norms. The function of social control is to assure that members of a group can carry out their essential activities (e.g., acquire food, shelter) without being constrained by the actions of others. Social control seeks to assure a minimum level of predictability in behavior and promote the well-being of the group as a whole. A central feature of informal social control is the development of social norms. Norms are prescriptions for proper behavior which develop in a social group. At the societal level, for example, norms include respecting the person and property of others. At the neighborhood level, they may include maintaining property, no public consumption of alcohol and the like.

Social control can take two basic forms: formal and informal. Formal social control is based on written rules or laws and prescribed punishments for breaking these rules or laws. In society, the police and courts are charged with maintaining formal social control. In contrast, informal social control is not based on laws or other written rules, but on custom or common agreement. Here it is citizens who enforce these norms, although the police may also be involved. The sanctions applied to violators are sometimes subtle such as verbal reprimand, rejection, embarrassment, or sometimes less subtle such as warnings and threats. This informal system may also invoke the formal system in dealing with security and quality of life issues in a neighborhood. Suspicion of external institutions inhibits some neighborhoods from invoking the aid of outside institutions.

Informal social control in the neighborhood context refers primarily to the enforcement of local rules for appropriate public behavior. As James Q. Wilson states, informal control is

the observance of standards of right and seemly conduct in the public places in which one lives and moves, those standards to be consistent

---

*Reprinted with editorial adaption from Greenberg, Rohe & Williams. *Informal Citizen Action and Crime Prevention at the Neighborhood Level.* Wash, D.C.: U. S. Department of Justice, 1985.

with—and supportive of—the values and life styles of the particular neighborhood.

Informal social control ranges on a continuum according to the formality of the organizational structure (see Figure 1). At the least formal end of the continuum is the individual acting alone or with the primary peer group. In this case, social control is exercised through direct confrontation or more subtle peer pressure such as a raised eyebrow, gossip, or ridicule. Roughly in the middle would be a group of neighbors getting together to address a specific problem, like a local teenager who is causing trouble in the neighborhood. The group does not have a name, does not really think of itself as a group or hold regular meetings, and has no purpose other than to address the problem immediately at hand. At the most formal end of the informal part of the continuum are neighborhood organizations. They typically have names, hold regular meetings, often have officers, and are usually formed to address a general (rather than a specific) problem, like crime, housing, or youth unemployment. Neighborhood organizations have the potential to exercise social control. Through various group activities, they can help to define and reinforce informal norms for acceptable public behavior. Clean-up and beautification programs, for example, set a certain standard for property maintenance. These organizations can also help to enforce formal laws by promoting citizen reporting of crimes to the police, lobbying public officials to improve protection, and hiring security personnel and private police.

Figure 1
Forms of Social Control

FORMAL	INFORMAL		
Police and courts enforce official laws	Neighborhood organization pressure to conform to norms	Informal ad hoc group pressure to conform to norms	Individual or peer group pressure to conform to norms

National experience with crime prevention indicates that formal means of social control are limited in their ability to control crime by the manpower available and by the inability of the police to always be where the crimes are being committed. Informal social control by citizens may offer a means of supplementing formal social control and helping to reduce crime and fear in the neighborhood. Neighbors can go beyond simply reporting crimes they observe and can actually deter crime by establishing norms for behavior and enforcing them through the various mechanisms discussed above (e.g., gossip, scolding surveillance). In essence, they are creating an atmosphere in which unruly or criminal behavior is not tolerated.

A second reason informal social control is important in crime prevention is that it underlies many of the more formal approaches to community crime prevention. Community Watch programs, for example, often promote informal social control through activities designed to acquaint neighbors with one another and to encourage intervention in suspected crimes. A better understanding of what informal social control is, and how it can be developed or supported, should help in the design of these programs.

Finally, a fuller understanding of informal social control should provide new ideas for and approaches to reducing crime. Since most of the attention has been focused on more organized means of social control, a closer look at the less organized means may provide new approaches to crime reduction.

A central element of informal social control is that it involves groups of people establishing and enforcing norms. Both theory and research indicate that the more cohesive a group, the more effective it is in generating informal social control. This generally applies to the control of both group members and outsiders. The more committed a group member is, the more likely he or she will conform to group norms and be affected by group sanctions such as ridicule or rejection. Similarly, more cohesive groups are better able to respond to threats by outsiders. They are less likely to give up or disintegrate in the face of an external threat (e.g., crimes committed by outsiders) and more likely to adopt protective actions.

Several factors have been identified as contributing to the formation of informal social groups and to their cohesiveness. The most basic appears to be the frequency of social contacts. The more contacts among individuals in a group, the more likely it is that an informal social group will form. Some similarity in beliefs, interests and/or social characteristics — such as ethnicity, race, religion, and economic status — is also necessary. However, most neighbors share an interest in maintaining a safe neighborhood, but other similarities, such as socioeconomic status, may be necessary for informal groups to form.

Two other factors associated with group formation and cohesion are physical proximity and group size. Physical proximity and visual accessibility between neighbors has been found to be the basis for the development of social groups in residential settings. Moreover, for an informal group to remain cohesive, it must stay small. As it grows larger, the face-to-face interactions grow fewer, and the group tends to break apart or to evolve into a more formal organization with written rules and regulations.

The literature on informal social control leads us to several major conclusions. First, informal social control must be viewed as a continuum for primary peer group pressure to the activities of neighborhood organizations. Second, the activities of informal groups may have an important influence on the crime rate in the local area. Third, informal social control depends on the existence of cohesive social groups, the strength of which depends upon the amount of social interaction, similarity of residents on socioeconomic attitudinal dimensions, physical and visual proximity, and group size.

Although there is only limited evidence, it appears that the major influence of informal social control on crime is through its impact on the perceptions of potential offenders. Studies have found, for example, that visibility and the presence of potential witnesses discourage potential offenders from victimizing person or destroying property. Furthermore, the practitioners at the workship felt that informal social control has an indirect effect on serious crime. Participants believed that in areas where there are strong visible signs of control and mutual responsibility (e.g., well-kept yards, extensive social interaction among neighbors), potential offenders feel that they are more likely to be detected and reported to the police. Potential offenders, therefore, tend to look elsewhere to commit crimes or decide not to commit the crime at all. Particular areas may also develop a reputation for intolerance to crime which also serves as a deterrent.

Although there is some evidence that informal social control has an effect on rates of serious crime it is not conclusive. To a large extent, this is because the measures of informal social control have been poor. Many researchers studying this topic have not actually measured informal social control but, rather, have measured the social or physical characteristics of neighborhoods that are believed to affect informal social control or the variables that are believed to encourage the exercise of informal social control such as local ties, neighborhood attachments, perceptions or control over the neighborhood or the ability to recognize strangers.

The findings of these studies indicate that having friends in the neighborhood, neighboring activities and the ability to recognize strangers are *not* related to crime rates. Emotional attachment to the neighborhood, perceived responsibility for and control over the neighborhood, the expressed willingness of a resident to intervene in a criminal event, and the belief that neighbors would also intervene in a criminal event *are* associated with low crime rates. Emotional attachment and perceptions of control, however, may be an effect of area crime rates and not a cause. That is, crime rates may not be lowered by a sense of commitment and control; rather, such feelings may be promoted by living in a low crime area.

Other evidence comes from studies of how social characteristics of neighborhoods are related to crime rates. High crime rates have been found to be associated with low economic status, a high proportion of minorities, ethnic and class heterogeneity, transience, and a high ratio of teens to adults. One common interpretation of these findings is that these areas are socially disorganized and lacking in social cohesion and, as a result, are unable to exercise informal social control over insiders or outsiders. Another interpretation of the high crime rates in these neighborhoods, however, is that the frustration caused by having few opportunities for high income, a steady job, prestige, and the like causes people to seek illegitimate means of acquiring money and possessions. In addition, since low-income transient neighborhoods usually have a fair amount of commercial activity (e.g., grocery stores, liquor stores, bars), there are also more opportunities for crime, particularly property crime. Thus, there are other explanations for crime in these neighborhoods, and we cannot safely conclude that the high crime rate is the result of a lack of informal social control.

The defensible space literature also provides some evidence for the importance of informal social control. Defensible space is the popular term for the idea that certain design characteristics of buildings and neighborhoods can reinforce informal social control by encouraging people to adopt a sense of responsibility over the spaces around their homes. Defensible space designs typically include smaller buildings with fewer floors; entrance ways that serve a small number of units; hallways, stairways, and entranceway designs that allow easy surveillance; the use of markers to define and differentiate public and private areas; and other features designed to encourage informal social control and limit or discourage access by outsiders. The evidence supporting the relationship between informal social control and physical design is mixed and, in general, studies have found that economic level and social homogeneity have a greater effect on the sense of informal social control and responsibility than do physical characteristics. This is not to say that physical design features are not related to crime, only that there is little clear evidence that they do so by affecting the strength of informal social control.

The final course of evidence on the effect of informal social control on serious crime is research on actual intervention in crimes. The numerous newspaper accounts of bystanders intervening in crimes (or not intervening, as in the famous Kitty Genovese case where a woman was stabbed to death while 38 people looked on and took no action) has led researchers to study the conditions under which people come to the aid of others. Studies have found that witnesses are more likely to offer direct assistance or report the problem to the police if they know other witnesses or the victim, or if they are familiar with the place in which the event occurred. This suggests that if people know their neighbors and their neighborhoods, they are more likely to intervene in crimes, assist victims, or report the crime to the police. But, in fact, the opportunities for directly intervening in a crime or reporting it to the police are probably rare, and the degree to which these interventions have an effect on future crime rates in the area is uncertain.

In conclusion, although there is no totally convincing evidence that informal social control does have an influence on serious crime rates, most evidence points in this direction.

Beyond its direct negative consequences, crime also increases fear levels among neighborhood residents. This fear can lead to the withdrawal of residents into fortified homes and to decisions to move to what are seen as safe areas. This in turn further weakens informal social controls. Research has shown, however, that fear levels do not always correspond with actual risk of being victimized. Hence, in crime control programs, it is important to address fear of crime as well as actual crime.

In the last few years, two explanations of fear have been developed: the victimization perspective and the social control perspective. According to the victimization perspective, a high crime rate leads to high risk of victimization which, in turn, leads to a high level of fear. According to the social control perspective, fear is viewed as a response not only to crime but to the deterioration of social control in the community. This deterioration may be the result of a sense of general decline in the quality of community life, an absence of social support networks or organizational resources to deal with local problems, loss of confidence in the economic stability of the neighborhoods, conflict between class or ethnic groups living in the same neighborhoods, or concern that new-comers in the neighborhood are destroying the social fabric. The social control perspective puts more emphasis on the causes of crime than does the victimization perspective.

Research findings support both the victimization and the social control perspective. Supporting the victimization perspective is the finding that levels of fear generally correspond with neighborhood crime rates, and victimization (of either oneself or someone else in the household) increases fear. Yet, other crime-related factors have been found to be much more important than area crime levels or victimization in explaining fear. Women and the elderly, two groups with the lowest risk of most types of victimization, express the highest levels of fear. Fear among these groups appears to lead to greater protective behavior, such as staying in at night, which reduces victimization. Vicariously experiencing the victimization of others in the neighborhood has also been found to increase fear.

Supporting the social control perspective are studies that have found that the greater the sense of responsibility and control over what goes on in the neighborhood, the lower the level of fear. By the same token, the greater the number of nuisance problems perceived in the neighborhood (e.g., litter, vacant lots, teens hanging out on corners) and the weaker the confidence in the economic future of the neighborhood, the higher the fear. People who believe that their neighborhood is a good investment and who are satisfied with the quality of housing tend to express low fear, even in neighborhoods with relatively high crime rates. People who lack confidence in the economic viability of the neighborhood may feel vulnerable to various problems that are believed to be beyond their control: one such problem may be victimization. These findings indicate that neighborhood characteristics that are not directly related to crime such as the physical condition of housing, are relevant to fear.

Although there is little conclusive evidence that informal social control influences serious crime, evidence from a number of different sources points in this direction. Based on the strength of both the statistical evidence and the observations of practitioners, we believe that attempts to strengthen informal social control should be a part of comprehensive crime prevention strategies. We would not recommend, however, that this be the only approach adopted. Furthermore, we know that the greater the familiarity with the place and the people involved, the more likely people are to intervene in a crime. Neighborhood Watch and other citizen-based crime prevention can do much to establish familiarity, when this is set as a specific goal of the program. If programs are designed to encourage intervention, however, guidelines for determining the nature of the intervention (e.g., reporting, verbal involvement, physical involvement) should be established to help protect residents.

The research findings further highlight the importance of local physical conditions and nuisance crimes in portraying an image of a lack of informal social control and safety. Although there is no evidence that nuisance crimes are related to more serious crimes, they have been associated with higher fear levels. Addressing these nuisance crimes should also be a part of a comprehensive crime prevention program. Neighborhood organizations can do much to address these problems by sponsoring neighborhood improvement activities and lobbying city officials to enforce vagrancy laws, increase police presence, and improve public facilities in the area. These groups can also strengthen the image of informal social control by erecting physical or symbolic barriers, organizing citizen patrols and developing a reputation for not tolerating criminal activities.

Research suggests that programs to reduce fear should approach the task by (1) instituting programs designed to reduce actual crime levels and (2) instituting programs designed to increase informal social control and helping networks. It is important to employ both strategies to avoid developing the false sense of security among residents which may occur if fear reduction programs were developed without crime reduction strategies.

Chapter 6

PROTECTING THE CHILDREN

Children are precious and vulnerable to sexual attack, but not necessarily helpless. They are destined to be sexual targets, but not predestined to be victims. Parental recognition of the susceptibility of children to attack, together with the application of prudent security principles, can go a long way toward safeguarding young people. Central to the issue of prevention is an understanding of the nature and setting of sex assaults on children, which are described in some depth in Chapter 6. It will do well to briefly review that information.

Sexual attacks by strangers usually occur in the summer months, in daylight, outdoors, in a park or in a vehicle, or inside of or near a public building. It is almost always a single encounter with a male, whom the victim has never seen and will never see again, unless there is an arrest. Conversely, acquaintance assault most often occurs in the home of the victim or attacker. The perpetrators are almost always men involved in a heterosexual attack on a g rl. Attacks generally recur, sometimes over long periods of time.

Although other topics are discussed in this chapter, the primary focus is on the protection of children from sexual assault. However, the techniques addressed herein have wider application than just the safeguarding of young people from sexual attack. A protective strategy aimed at this end also shields children from other forms of physical abuse, as well as abduction. Before proceeding with the discussion of security, a word of caution is in order.

Protection vs. Overprotection

If two parents were to create a strategy for making their children 100 percent safe from crime, they probably could succeed, with some minor side effects: they would ruin their children's lives and ensure a disastrous adulthood. Complete preoccupation with a child's safety, coupled with an attempt to utterly insulate him or her from criminal assault, however laudable the goal, would create an environment so stifling, so over-protective, so isolated from normal human encounters that emotional growth and development would be profoundly retarded.

In some communities, concern for the safety of children has reached near frenzy. Incidents such as the kidnapping and murder of Adam Walsh, the publicity surrounding serial murderers who preyed on children, as well as the cacophony of warnings from newly-formed child advocacy organizations to protect children from abduction and assault, have created an environment of fear among parents, fear that is being transmitted to kids. Local disclosures of adult sexual misconduct seem to be reported by the press with a curious form of enthusiasm: the married scoutmaster who assaulted his charges for a decade; the little league coach who molested a neighbor's six-year old daughter; the bank president who fondled his babysitter; the teacher who sexually abused a seven-year old student. Can no one be trusted? Perhaps not; however, the answer is prudent precautions, not hysteria. In raising a child, safety and security must be first considerations, but not the only ones. Consider what experts say about the growth and development of children.

Erikson has subdivided the life of humans into eight developmental periods, each of which has definable goals and objectives. These, the "eight stages of man," are:

1. Infancy (first year of life)
2. Early childhood (one to six years of age)
3. Middle childhood (six to nine)
4. Preadolescence (nine to twelve)
5. Adolescence (thirteen to twenty)
6. Early adulthood (twenty-one to forty-five)
7. Middle-age (forty-five to sixty-five)
8. Aging (over sixty-five)

Note that fully half of the stages are reached during the first nine years of life, and only two periods occur over the last 25 to 30 years. That means, of course, that children are constantly growing, changing, learning, evolving. Many scholars believe that parents' main job is to lovingly assist children in their quest for independence. In each period of life, humans, if they can be expected to ascend to the next developmental stage intact and on schedule, must achieve certain objectives. For example, the early childhood years, a stage that stretches from the end of infancy to about six years of age, has definable objectives. Developmentally, the following tasks should be met by the child, with adult guidance: (1) achieving independence in self-care; (2) learning sex-differences; (3) forming concepts of reality; (4) developing perceptions of right and wrong (ethics); and (5) identifying with parents, siblings and significant others.

These developmental tasks are hurdles that children must clear in order to satisfy the emotional growth requirements associated with early childhood. They are also consistent with a *prudent* program of security designed to protect youngsters in that category from crime, as long as that protection is not so overwhelming that it blocks the growth process. A social scientist once wrote:

> Fear is a handicapping emotion. There is a predisposition to fear certain things, but typically fears are learned. Eighty percent of five year olds reported they were afraid of wild animals or snakes. One-third of children below age seven were afraid of imaginary things ... maturity increases the logic of fears, but the reflection of the home atmosphere and parental anxiety persists.

Most fear, then, is learned, and it can be very destructive if it hinders growth. Furthermore, an environment that is so controlled that it retards development, even though it physically protects children from harm, is an expensive tradeoff emotionally. The answer is *balance;* a program of security that decreases a child's vulnerability to crime, while recognizing that he or she also must grow as a human being. In effect, adults must know about children—and childhood—as a first step in balancing a child's emotional needs with his or her requirements for safety. The attempt to protect a child without overprotecting him or her is more an art than a science, but it cannot be done in a climate of fear or hysteria or in a home that dwells endlessly on the world's wickedness.

Educate the Child—and Yourself

Any strategy designed to safeguard children from attack begins with conversation and communication. It is difficult for many parents to discuss sex with their children, must less sexual assaultsm yet these topics must be discussed. There exists in many people an embarrassment over things sexual, partially because it is supposed to be the most private of subjects and partly because they were not properly oriented to the subject when they were children. A good human sexuality book, appropriate to the age of the child to be instructed, should be obtained and read by a parent prior to any attempt at instruction.

A parent should first find out how much a child knows about sex and sexual assault. If the child knows nothing, then he or she should be told about these subjects. If he or she does know something about one or both phenomena, it is time for the parent to be a good listener. Find out what is known and *where it was learned*. Sexual misconceptions should be corrected prior to proceeding with information which is new to the child.

The child should be told about his or her body: the parts, bodily functions, sexuality. Labelling of the body parts should be accurate, not terms of slang or euphemisms. A penis is not "pee pee," it is a penis. Once they have a basic understanding of their bodies, children should be informed that their body belongs to them alone and that they have a right to resist *anyone's* attempts to touch or feel them. In short, forced sexual contact is not something they should feel compelled to submit to. A good idea is to devise a short but effective phrase that can be easily memorized by children and repeated to adults whom they wish to discourage from touching them (e.g., "Please don't touch me; I don't like it.").

In concert with that advice, they must be informed that a few people may try to hurt them, or trick or threaten them into submitting to sexual advances. It should be explained that although most people are decent and trustworthy, they must be watchful for those who are not. A child's reaction to sexual advances should be twofold and cannot be over-emphasized by parents: Say "no," and tell your parents right away.

The U. S. Department of Health and Human Services goes even further with its advice because of studies which document the frequency of acquaintance assaults. It counsels:

> Tell your child that adults whom they know, trust and love who might be in a position of authority (like a babysitter, an uncle, or even a policeman) might try to do something like this. Try not to scare your children—emphasize that the vast majority of grownups never do this and that most adults are deeply concerned about protecting them from harm.

Children should also be told that some attackers are subtle; they don't directly assault children, but preceed attacks with gifts, offers to help and unsolicited favors. Some pre-assaultive conditions involve suggestive or pornographic pictures, and touching. The child's response: say "no" and tell your parents right away. The customary advice of "don't talk to strangers," "don't take candy from strangers" and "don't accept rides," is still sound, but insufficient.

If children are taught to be slavishly obedient to adults then it will be difficult to teach them to say "no" when they should. Instead, although respect for authority and obedience to parents and significant others are virtues, children who are independent and curious are more likely to resist and report abuse than those who are trained to blindly follow orders.

The youngster should be asked to identify what in his or her mind are perilous situations. Leading questions—questions that suggest an answer—should be avoided by parents, who are trying to discover what children perceive to be dangerous and why—*in their own words*. A way to ask such a question is: "What are the three things that you are most afraid of?" The wrong way to proceed is to ask: "Are you afraid of the dark?" Once the answer is given it should be determined whether the child has encountered these feared situations or whether they know someone who has.

While traditional role playing may not be appropriate for very young children, it will be helpful to pose hypothetical ("What if . . . ") questions to them which are aimed at evaluating their perception of danger and their response to it. An example of such a hypothetical: "What would you do if a man you did not know told you at your school bus stop that your mom had asked him to drive you home?" It might be wise to add elements to each hypothetical after the child's initial answer—assuming the answer is, "I wouldn't go with him"—such as, " . . . but what if the man insists that you go, and he knows mom's name and where she works and where you live?" Life is not a true-false game, and neither should be these exercises. They stimulate thinking, critical decision-making, discrimination between alternatives, while reinforcing desired responses to potentially dangerous encounters.

Hypothetical questions, and the dialogue that accompanies them, are effective instructional techniques that can be used to convey a variety of messages on everything from bicycle safety to home security, protection against fire to personal security. They take some planning by parents, but they are of great value. Youngsters' attention spans being what they are, repetition is essential.

Once a child becomes comfortable with the hypothetical format, he or she should be confronted with more difficult situations, those involving questions of what to do if an attack is imminent or even in-progress. Remember, the life of a child is too important to encourage heroics, so youngsters should be told to avoid encounters and locations that may lead to assault, but if one occurs remain calm, flee if possible but do not resist unless there is a good chance for escape, and remember as much about the attacker (clothing, physical description, etc.) and his vehicle as possible.

It is especially important to offset negative stereotypes which may lead to victimization. For instance, if a female youngster is being raised in an environment that reinforces the concept of male dominance and supe-riority, then that family may be raising a *de facto* victim. Ideally, this ragged theory of male superiority should not be taught in the home. In any event, the most effective preventive strategy for young girls is to help them develop a strong sense of their worth as individuals, along with a belief that they have domain over their bodies and a right to say "no."

Not everyone who touches or displays affection for a child is a "pervert." It is a continuing tragedy that the present hysteria over sexual abuse has led to a fear among adults that affectionate behavior toward young people must be avoided lest it be misunderstood. Many elementary school teachers, for example, seem reluctant to express affection for their students because of the negative connotation associated with the simplest gestures of fondness. Parents must be alert, vigilant and concerned about the safety of their children, but not to the point of reacting prematurely to suspicions and making reckless accusations based on embryonic evidence. Suspicions should lead to calm investigations, not histrionics.

By way of summary, the education of children should involve the following:

1. A child should be told about his or her body, its function and human sexuality. Body parts should be properly identified by their correct names, not euphemisms.

2. A child's body belongs to that child and forced touching or feeling, by anyone, need not be permitted.

3. There are people who may try to force sexual attentions on children. Some of those people may even be friends or relatives.

4. Sexual attacks often begin indirectly, subtly, with pre-assaultive behavior that consists of gifts, offers to help, or displays of suggestive photographs.

5. Initial parental conversations with children should elicit what they know about sex and sexual abuse and where they learned it.

6. Youngsters should be asked to identify what they consider dangerous situations. Leading questions should not be used.

7. Hypothetical questions are a valuable tool for teaching critical thinking, and for presenting situations to a child which may someday have to be confronted.

8. Negative sex stereotypes about male superiority should be avoided. Girls should be encouraged to develop a strong self-concept, as well as an understanding that they have every right to say "no" to sexual advances.

9. Not all displays of affection (e.g.—touching, hugging, etc.) are attempts at sexual abuse. In fact, most are merely gestures of fondness. Suspected abuse should be calmly investigated before accusations are made or inferred.

There is no optimum age that a child should reach before the educational process, at least as it relates to security, is undertaken. The best judges of this threshold are parents. Still, individual differences notwithstanding, instructions should commence well before kindergarten, perhaps even by the second year.

Establishing the Rules

The general education of a child just discussed is an important first step in protecting a young person against criminal attack. There is, however, a need to establish and enforce other rules that must be strictly obeyed by youngsters. The child's early orientation can be thought of as "basic training," so it may be helpful to think of the following twenty tenets as "continuing education." The National Crime Prevention Council has prepared an excellent list of comprehensive security instructions for children, which have been modified, adapted and enlarged for this volume. The following advice to young children is strongly recommended; and should be repeated often:

- Never accept rides, candy, gifts, money or medicine from a stranger—anyone you do not know well
- Never get close to a car if a stranger calls out to you for directions or anything else. It is easy for a stranger to pull you into a car
- Never give your name and address, or anyone else's name or address, to a stranger
- Never open the door of your home to anyone you do not know
- Never tell telephone callers that you are home alone. Take messages and tell them mom or dad is busy and will call back

- Never volunteer information about family vacation plans or information about your home
- Always avoid strangers who seem to be hanging around restrooms or playgrounds and want to play with you or your friends
- If a stranger in a car bothers you, turn away and run in the opposite direction—it is difficult for a car to change direction suddenly
- When frightened, run to the nearest person you can find, especially a police officer, a worker, a man or woman in a business or store, or someone in a nearby house. While you should avoid strangers who approach you, it is fine to ask an adult you do not know for help if you are scared or lost
- If a stranger tries to follow you on foot or tries to grab you, run away, scream and make lots of noise because bad strangers are frightened of noise and attention
- Never play in deserted areas such as the woods, a parking lot, an alley, empty buildings or new construction sites
- Always stick to the same route to and from school or a friend's house (note: parents should pick the route)
- Always try to play or walk with friends because it is safer and more fun that way
- Never play or loiter around restrooms, elevators stairwells or laundry rooms
- When you take a bus, try to sit near the driver
- Never display money in public
- Never hitchhike under any circumstances
- Make sure you know your address and telephone number
- Never walk or play alone at or just before dark
- Whenever you leave home it is necessary that you tell a family member where you are going and when you will be back

While there is no substitute for common sense, children who are equipped with a complete list of do's and don'ts have a firm basis for the application of common sense. The above list may not be all-inclusive, but it is a good start and should be taught and strictly enforced.

Neighborhood Programs

There is collective action that neighbors can take to maximize the safety of children. A good way to proceed with a community program is to contact local law enforcement authorities for assistance or advice in setting one up. Some police departments have extensive strategies and plans for community crime prevention; others have none. In any event, some of the most popular schemes follow, some of which can be initiated without police assistance.

Fingerprinting and Photographing Children

A growing number of police departments, often in conjunction with schools, are fingerprinting and photographing young children as a way of identifying them in times of crisis. While this is not a crime prevention tool *per se,* it does serve as a way of facilitating the identification of youngsters should they be abducted or injured.

Safe Homes

Homeowners or renters in a discernable neighborhood are asked, as a part of this program, to utilize their residences as a kind of home base, in which children who are lost, frightened or are fleeing from a real or perceived attack can seek temporary sanctuary. Signs are posted in windows that can be clearly seen by youngsters. These are also places to which latch key children can go in the time of need.

Block Patrols

Organized patrols, as the name denotes, are neighbors who patrol, either on foot or in vehicles, an area frequented by children at times of most vulnerability, such as immediately before or right after school. Some patrols may work closely with the police; others will operate more or less independently. This program is a true crime prevention program that seeks to deter crime rather than react to it after it occurs.

Public School Programs

Increasingly, public schools have begun to undertake responsibilities, not just for a child's education, but for his or her safety. School crime watches now abound, as well as crime prevention curricula designed to make youngsters more aware of their personal safety. Police officers lecture in schools and teaching aids, such as puppets, coloring books and posters, are used to make lessons more effective. Parents are also enlisted in the process. Programs such as "parent alert," in which volunteers call the parents of absent children to check on their safety, are gaining widespread acceptance.

As with all programs, parents must make an effort to find out what is available in their community. However, the absence of a desired program does not mean that a small group of motivated parents cannot create it with or without official support.

Choosing a Preschool or Day Care Center

Day care has been in the news. Within one six-month period, a series of scandals occurred in various sections of the country in which employees of day care centers were arrested with depressing regularity for sexually assaulting the children they were paid to supervise. As a result, peoples' confidence in the industry was shaken, as state after state moved swiftly to upgrade standards, toughen licensure requirements and step up on-site inspections. The industry will survive this period of controversy, mostly because the service it offers is becoming increasingly essential to a society in which women choose or are forced to work. But, regardless of how tough a state's oversight laws are, it is incumbent on parents to perform their own on-site investigations of a day care facility and personnel so that they may determine whether it is the type of place to which they should entrust their sons and daughters during one of lifes most vulnerable and impressionable stages. Following are some tips on how to go about selecting a day care center. While there are no ironclad guarantees that children will be completely protected from harm if parents put the principles to work, the suggestions do represent a prudent attempt to maximize the likelihood of a correct decision.

Every state has an agency or agencies that are supposed to regulate — even license or register — day care centers. In some states, the rules are extensive and the oversight is close, while in others, regulations may be superficial and supervision occasional, at best. One of the first steps to be taken in selecting a center is to determine which local, county or state agencies are responsible for regulating day care, and what they can tell you about the center you are considering, including what was seen when inspectors last visited the facility.

When a parent makes an initial visit to a day care center, it should be at a time when the children are there and active. Every room and location in the facility should be inspected. Is the place clean, cheerfully decorated and well prepared and equipped? The owner and director should be interviewed. How long has he been in the business? What are their backgrounds? How long has this center been in operation and how long have they been with the center? How many children attend the facility? How many staff members are there? The U. S. Department of Health and Human Services recommends a child-staff ratio of four or five to one for children below the age of three, and no more than nine to one for children from three to five years old.

On the initial or follow-up visit, the parent should spend as much time as he or she can observing the interaction between staff and children. "Group size" (the ratio of children to staff in any group or room), should not exceed twelve to one for children younger than three, and less than twenty to one for children three to five years old. Numbers in excess of these ratios may mean that youngsters are not being supervised closely enough and are thus less secure than they could be. Observe what activities take place during the visit. How do the children related to staff members and vice-versa? Ask a staff member, outside the hearing of any other employees, to give a summary of an average day's activities. Ask the director the same questions and compare the two answers. See if he will provide you with the names and telephone numbers of other parents whose children have been enrolled at the center for some time. They should be contacted for their opinions on the facility, and asked to furnish names of other parents, preferably ones that the director did not give.

The most important element of any day care operation is personnel. The success or failure of any facility is directly related to the quality of employees. Therefore, the employee selection process is a task of great importance to a center's mission. A parent who wishes to make a correct decision on whether to entrust children to the center must find as much out about the staff as possible, even if the premises is church-affiliated. Ask to see personnel files or the hiring folder of some employees, then make sure that the decision to hire a staff member was valid and reliable. Some states require background inquiries, fingerprinting and criminal record ("rap") checks on applicants for day care positions. If this is the case in your state, make sure it was done.

Parents who wish to evaluate the soundness of a day care center's hiring decisions may have trouble doing so unless they have some evaluative criteria. The Department Health and Human Services has published a brochure that contains suggested recruitment and selection rules for day care workers. These rules, which should be viewed as standards in the industry, can be utilized by a parent in determining whether a center has made proper personnel decisions. They are summarized below:

1. Any vacancy in a day care center should be filled from a pool of qualified applicants, preferably after the position has been advertised.

2. All candidates should fill out a comprehensive application form that contains spaces for name, address, telephone number, applicant's present job and reason for wanting to leave, educational achievements, work history, special skills, other accomplishments and references.

3. Candidates should be formally interviewed by prospective employers to determine their attitude and philosophy.

4. If possible, a prospective employee should be observed doing the kind of work for which they are applying.

5. A comprehensive background investigation of the applicant should be conducted in which all the data on the application form is validated. Any contact that the candidate has had with children and parents should be closely checked.

6. In contacting employment references the following questions should be asked and answered:

- How does the applicant relate to children?
- What was the applicant's attendance or absentee record?
- How well does the applicant accept responsibility?
- How well does the applicant get along with co-workers and supervisors?
- Is the applicant trustworthy and honest?
- What are the applicants strong and weak points?

7. In those states which allow it, a criminal background check should be accomplished either at the state or local level.

8. A newly hired employee should be closely supervised and placed on probation for a time after he or she is hired.

Every day care center should have a written code of conduct for staff members relative to the behavior of children (is physical punishment allowed?), policies on reporting child abuse or neglect to authorities, and procedures for investigating charges of staff misconduct. Ask to see these documents. They do not have to be sophisticated policies, but they should be in writing.

A center's policy on parental visitations should be determined. Parents should not only be permitted to visit a day care facility, they ought to be encouraged to do so. Any center which systematically attempts to dissuade parents from dropping in because it somehow interferes with "the work," should be viewed with suspicion. Consider the following statement by the Federal Office of Human Development Services on the monitering of new day care staff members:

> Monitering of the employee by parents is also important. Parents should be *encouraged* to drop in and visit the new employee.

In making a physical inspection of a day care facility, a parent should be alert for possible deficiencies that relate to the quality of care afforded. It is entirely possible for a parent with no background in the industry to determine with a reasonable degree of certainty whether certain fundamental precautions have been taken to safeguard children. The following questions have been suggested by the Federal Administration for Children, Youths and Families. It might be a good idea for parents to copy this page, which is done in checklist format, as a way of determining whether the day care center has:

	YES	NO
An up-to-date license?	☐	☐
A clean and comfortable look?	☐	☐
Enough space indoors and out so that all the children can move freely and safely?	☐	☐
A sufficient ratio of staff to children?	☐	☐
Enough furniture and playthings for all children?	☐	☐
Equipment that is safe and in good repair?	☐	☐
Equipment and material that is suitable for the ages of the children?	☐	☐
Enough rooms and facilities for naps?	☐	☐
Clean and sufficient bathroom facilities?	☐	☐
Safety caps on electrical outlets?	☐	☐
A safe place to store medicine, household, cleansers, poison, matches, sharp instruments?	☐	☐
Fire exits plainly marked?	☐	☐
A safety plan in case of emergencies?	☐	☐
An outdoor play area that is safe, fenced, free of litter and supervised?	☐	☐
Enough heat, air conditioning, light and ventilation?	☐	☐
Nutritious meals and snacks made of the kinds of food you approve of?	☐	☐
A separate, supervised room for sick children?	☐	☐

A comprehensive first aid kit?   □   □

Fire extinguishers?   □   □

Smoke detectors?   □   □

Covered and protected heaters?   □   □

Strong screens or bars on windows above the first floor?   □   □

This checklist is a general one, but the survey is a good way to undertake a systematic first analysis of day care.

Parental monitoring of the facility should continue through a child's enrollment. Get involved and stay involved! If work or other committments do not permit such involvement, perhaps it would be possible to attend evening meetings or to solicit information on a continuing basis from another parent who can devote more time to visitations.

Some parental concerns about a child's safety can be addressed in advance. For example, the center's director can be instructed that the child should never be left alone, or that the child should not be transported in any vehicle unless prior permission is given. Furthermore, it should be communicated in writing to the center, the people (if any) to whom the child may be released other than the enrolling parent or parents. Additional do's and don'ts should be thought out by parents based on their individual situations.

Daily conversation should be initiated with children who attend day care as a way of monitering their activities. Youngsters should be encouraged to share their experiences, including the relationships they have developed with staff members and peers. Most day care centers are reputable businesses and most employees are good people. Parents must be vigilant for the exceptions.

In-Home Care

Very few American families have not made use of some form of in-home care of children whether it has been a live-in housekeeper or an occasional babysitter. This is an important service and, given the data on sexual abuse of children which indicates the significant number of assaults which occur in the home, one that needs to be carefully controlled and closely supervised.

Every potential in-home caregiver, with the possible exception of relatives, should be interviewed, either formally or informally. In the case of housekeepers and sitters who are not well-known to the parents, a formal interview is called for. References are essential, preferably from people who have seen the applicant in home situations, with children. There cannot be too many references, only too few. They should date back as far as possible, though this will be difficult in the case of teenage babysitters, who may be checked through neighbors, teachers, relatives and peers.

People who are inexperienced at interviewing tend to make a critical mistake: they speak when they should be listening. Ideally, an interview should start with enough small talk to make the parties comfortable with each other. Next, the parent should furnish the applicant with a *brief* statement of essentials about the job: how many children, ages and sexes, hours of work, pay, etc. Then, ask open-ended questions, (not leading questions) designed to determine the type of person you are facing. Do not *tell* them what sort of individual you are looking for. Most people who want the job will cheerfully acknowledge that they are precisely what you need. The Department of Health and Human Services recommends the following questions:

- What kinds of television programs do you think children should watch?
- What activities do you do with children?
- What do you do when a child disobeys?
- What do you do when you get angry at a child?
- What are some things you do with children to help them learn?
- How do you feel about combining housework with care?

It is altogether appropriate that an applicant be asked if he/she has ever been convicted of a crime. The question should be posed directly, without apology, eye-to-eye; and it should be answered. This person will have access to your home and children, so the question is not intrusive. If an applicant refuses to answer it, or tries to evade it, or has no references, or gives references which cannot be contacted, then he/she must not be hired, regardless of how desperately a housekeeper or sitter is needed.

Once a hiring decision has been made, it may be a good idea to write down, in rough contract form, the conditions of employment. The agreement can be handwritten, with copies for both the parent and caregiver. It serves to formalize verbal understandings, impress on the employee the extent to which the parent views the task as important, and increase the probability that orders will be followed. The contract should include economic aspects such as hours and pay, as well as expected duties. Security-related provisions should also be written in, such as:

- Emergency plans in the event of accident, illness, fire, bad weather, etc.
- Telephone numbers and full names of both parents, doctor, hospital emergency room, police, neighbors and other persons to be notified in case of emergency.
- Agreements about visitors, phone calls (in-going and out-going), television, and radio.

In monitoring the caregiver's work, an innocuous deception by parents may be of value. When leaving the house for the day or evening, the parents should overestimate their expected return home by an hour or two. In other words, if one plans to be home by 11:00 p.m., tell the caregiver that it will be 12:30 a.m., thus allowing a truer picture of the home situation than might be obtained otherwise.

Monitering Children for Problems

The times of a child's greatest vulnerability to criminal assault occur when he or she is alone, or with a single adult other than a parent, or with one other child, or in a public place with loose supervision. Recognition by parents of these four times of potential crisis can go a long way toward minimizing risks. First, it should be assured that when a child is with an adult, it is a person whom a parent has determined is trustworthy. Second, if two children of the tender years are together, they should be supervised closely, but as unobtrusively as possible, to afford them some privacy, without total isolation from oversight. Third, when a young child is in public, whether with parents or with anyone else, it is absolutely crucial that he or she is never out of line of sight supervision by a person of responsibility.

If this chapter has a single theme, it is that two-way communication between parents and children is an ironclad necessity, an important aspect of child rearing and an essential crime prevention tool. In the lives of children, the concept of prevention has two goals: take steps to ensure that a child is not victimized by crime; and, attempt to lessen the impact of victimization by detecting it as soon as possible, then putting a stop to it promptly. On the second point, communicating with youngsters, together with visual observations of their physical condition, behavior and even clothing, can detect a crime in its fledling stage so that intervention may be undertaken.

According to a study of children who were attacked sexually, but did not report those attacks, their refusal was based on *fear*. This fear took four forms: (1) fear that parents would punish them; (2) fear that parents would not believe their story; (3) fear that parents would reject or abandon them; and (4) fear that they could not adequately communicate the attack to parents, partly because they didn't know the right words to use in describing it. If, prior to an attack, a child has been warned it can happen, is convinced he can trust and rely on parents for support, understands his or her body, and has been equipped with a basic vocabulary, fear of disclosure is not likely.

In addition to interpersonal communication, parents should watch for physical and behavioral changes in a child, changes which may be symptomatic of criminal attack. Behaviorally, any profound variations should be investigated, including sleep disorders, loss of appetite, bedwetting, thumb sucking, unexplained weeping, problems in school, new fears, withdrawal from people, moodiness, extremes in behavior and phobias.

Any signs of physical injury, regardless of how minor, should be looked into, a time-consuming task since young children accumulate injuries the way philatelists collect stamps. Nonetheless, every scrape, every cut, every bruise, every bump, every limp, every swelling should be looked into, gently, in an understated way that connotes interest not suspicion. Clothing should be superficially examined before washings, especially undergarments, for unusual tears or stains.

Latch Key Children

Latch key children are youngsters who are alone at home, usually during the late afternoon hours, awaiting a parent's return from work. Many are products of divorce with working mothers. All of the suggestions that apply to other children apply to these young people, but they are in a special situation and therefore require special attention.

Parents should take reasonable precautions to allay a child's fears about being left alone. Fears are quite natural and will likely be more pronounced in the winter months because of the earlier onset of darkness. Relatively unrestricted access to radios and televisions supply calming diversions, despite the shallow nature of programming. Certain programs which might contribute to childhood fears should be banned by parents in advance. It would be nice if schoolwork could be completed during this time alone, and every attempt ought to be made to motivate a child to do it, though the primary parental concerns must be safety and absence of fear first, and task fulfillment second. Under no circumstances should a child be ridiculed for exhibiting fears about being alone.

The telephone is an important tool, not merely for its communication value, but because of the feeling of security it can give a child who is comforted that he has at least some access to help or company. The child should be delegated almost carte blanche access to the phone, though it would be a good idea to make him or her keep track of all outgoing calls. If a parent can be reached by phone, very few restrictions should be placed on the child unless it jeopardizes that parent's job. Repeated calls to the parent for little or no reason are the child's way of expressing discomfort with his or her situation. A list of important telephone numbers should be taped on or near the phone, in large letters. Within a half-hour after a child is due home, the parent should call and determine that he or she is there. In the case of incoming calls, a simple code might be worthwhile, such as two rings, hang-up and call back, in order to protect the youngster from threatening, obscene or annoying callers.

The child must be introduced to all the physical security aspects of the home: locks, alarms, window and door hardware, lights, etc. He should know how to operate them all. Door locks, especially auxilliary locks, should be placed so that a child can reach them without standing on a chair. He or she should also be instructed never to enter the home if it appears that there has been a break-in or some other type of unauthorized entry. There should be an alternate place to go under those circumstances.

Adequate food should be available so that the youngster will not be tempted to leave home, unless he or she is old enough to do so safely and is allowed to. Snacks should be prepared in advance by a parent so that no cooking, heating or cutting is necessary. If it is possible, neighbors who are usually home during the appropriate hours should be asked to check on the child.

There must be a strict policy on visitors which is clearly understood and followed. Careful consideration should be given to whether any non-supervisory visitors, such as another child, should be allowed in. In truth, two children are safer and less fearful then one, but they are often bolder and more inclined toward unruliness. Before making a decision to permit a visitor, the parent must balance the desirable results of allowing another child in with the possibility of negative consequences, which can be determined somewhat by the track record of the other child as well as the way in which the two kids act when they are together.

There can be some negative emotional consequences to being a young latch key child, one of which is that it pushes children into assuming responsibilities that are more appropriate for older kids, while making them more vulnerable to crime and the fears that accompany perceptions of isolation and powerlessness. Small gestures can go a long way toward alleviating these potential problems. For instance, instead of shopping for groceries on the way home from work, a parent should if possible come directly home, then go shopping, preferably with the child.

On the Police

A brief word about the way in which children should view police officers is altogether appropriate. Many people, children included, look on law enforcement officers with suspicion, cynicism and outright disdain. Some are even fearful of officers. These attitudes are not innate, they are learned, often from parents or other important adults. Great care should be taken by parents to impress upon children that police officers are allies, who have as one of their main functions the protection of people.

When a police officer is encountered by a parent and child, a few seconds should be taken to chat with the officer, most of whom appreciate the opportunity to speak with a citizen who respects them. At the very least, an officer should be verbally greeted. Books, even coloring books, or brochures which depict police officers in relatively sympathetic ways can be given to children. The idea here is not to portray officers as super heroes, but to convince children they can be relied on in times of trouble.

Something that police officers hate and parents should avoid is threats of arrest, however tongue in cheek, to compel children into obedience. The classic example, one that is often used in police academies to show recruits the hurdles they have to jump for community acceptance, is when a woman in a grocery store with a rebellious child points to a passing law enforcement officer and utters the words that make all officers cringe: "If you don't behave, that cop is going to arrest you." This inference, that the police are adversaries, is short-sighted and potentially dangerous. Parents should ask themselves whether they want a child who is in trouble to run toward or away from a police officer. Studious attention should be directed at instructing children that officers are there to help.

About Those Rock Concerts

Some questions about whether a mother should permit her children to attend rock concerts are easy to answer: if her twenty-six year old daughter in law school wants to go it is probably fine; if her ten year old fifth grader asks to attend one, it is probably not a good idea. It is the gap between these two examples that represents a large grey area, one this section may bring into sharper focus.

Rock concerts theoretically are nothing more than a forum for presenting music, but they are potential dangers to children. Chapter five contains a discussion of problems that have occurred at some concerts, difficulties that can be avoided in the future by parents and children with a little advanced preparation and some common sense.

A first parental step in determining whether a child should be permitted to attend a concert would be to listen to selections—both words and music—from the group in question to determine whether the message is alien to family values or to see if it promotes drugs, violence, sadism or anything else that might be inappropriate signals for children or that might contribute to a dangerous concert situation. It should be kept in mind that no "older generation" has ever given blanket approval to the music of its offspring, something parents who grew up under the insidious influence of Frank Sinatra, Elvis Presley or Mama Cass seem to forget. So, the idea here is not to look for utterly harmless music, but to be watchful for potential perils created by, for instance, heavy metal groups that pander to drug use and violence.

Parents may wish to accompany their children to a concert, a prospect most kids find unspeakably gross and demeaning, but something that can really serve to educate a parent. Young children, say those under the age of 16, really ought to be supervised by adults at concerts. It is the mid-teens (15 to 17 years) which present the toughest decisions, though it is generally a very bad idea for any young person to go to a performance alone. In making a judgement about whether a child should be allowed to attend a concert, the following factors should be considered.

1. Who is the group? Is it a heavy metal band or punk group preoccupied with drugs or mayhem? There is a world of difference between a Barry White and a Ted Nugent, and parents should understand such distinctions.

2. Where is the concert? Is it in a public or private auditorium? What is its reputation? Talk to parents who have allowed their children to attend prior concerts at the location.

3. How many people will be in attendance? Is the seating reserved? Or is there no seating available (i.e. "festival seating" or "sro")? Some parents do not permit their children to attend concerts unless seating is assigned and there are no gate sales, since riots have occurred at concerts that sold out with multitudes of enraged young people shut out of the show.

4. What security is provided, by whom, and how are security personnel deployed? Are cursory gate searches conducted? Some promoters hire security officers (so-called "t-shirt" security, since that is the extent of their uniform and training), police officers or a combination of both. Find out what kind, how many, and how they are dispersed. This last point is quite important. A promoter may proudly proclaim that he has hired 50 guards and 25 police officers; however, fully half the "t-shirt" may be assigned to protect the band from fans, with fifteen of the remaining personnel assigned to the turnstiles, leaving only ten to patrol the auditorium, which could be filled with 15,000 screaming fans, at least some of whom it can be guaranteed will be high on drugs or alcohol. It is not at all unusual to find that in some locales police officers *never* go into an auditorium during a performance because of the violent response their presence provokes from the crowd. Instead, officers will patrol parking lots or just stand-by in case they are needed.

5. With whom exactly do the children plan to go to the concert and are

they assured of sitting together? A group of young people takes on a personality of its own, and parents should be acquainted with the people who propose to accompany their children.

6. What is the mode of transportation to and from the concert? If it is by car, who will drive?

This information should be obtained, not by a child, but by parents, directly from a promoter or auditorium manager. If the above questions cannot be answered, the child should not be allowed to go.

If, however reluctantly, a parent decides to let a son or daughter attend a rock concert, a few basic rules should be laid down, from which any departure must be viewed in the harshest of terms. Rock concerts are potentially volatile gatherings, places where arrests are made, drug use is often rampant, injuries and overdoses are commonplace and crowd behavior is unpredictable. So parental instructions should be obeyed.

If youngsters are driving to a concert, they should leave well before the start of the performance, since these events often have traffic tie-ups of epic proportions. If valet parking is available and affordable, it should be used inasmuch as parking lots that serve concert facilities may be plagued with problems that range from larceny to sexual assault.

When young people go in a group, they should stay in that group throughout the concert and the trip. Everyone should carry some form of personal identification and be willing to produce it upon demand, especially to law enforcement officers. Articles such as jewelry, radios, tape recorders and cameras should be left at home. Food and drinks should be purchased only from official concessionaires to avoid "spiked" consumables. Children should be told not to stand on chairs or dance in the aisles, regardless of what other attendees do.

It will be quite impossible to enforce some of the recommended rules, so trust is essential if parents are to permit their children to attend concerts. If young people are untrustworthy or cannot be relied upon to exercise sound judgment, then they should be allowed to frequent rock concerts at about the same time they begin to make home mortgage payments.

Conclusion

Children are tempting targets for criminal attack but their vulnerability may be lessened through a recognition of the nature and extent of the problem, by parents who have at their disposal a myriad of strategies designed to "harden the target." However, great care must be exercised to ensure that young people are not so protected from assaults that their development as human beings is stifled. Accordingly, knowledge of a child's emotional needs, developmental tasks, and the destructive nature of fear, is a first parental step in devising a plan to protect youngsters.

Open communication between parent and child is essential. A child should be educated about his or her body, including the precise names and function of body parts. Children should be taught that they have a right to say "no" to sexual advances, and must report such activities to parents. The use of hypothetical questions ("what if") are an invaluable teaching aid in preparing children for incidents that everyone hopes they will not have to face. Since basic signs of affection, such as hugging, are not in and of themselves assaultive, great restraint must be practiced by parents before making damaging accusations against anyone.

Basic rules—do's and don'ts—should be established for children, and enforced to the letter. These guidelines are directed at protecting children outside the home when they are most vulnerable. Furthermore, neighborhood programs, such as the fingerprinting of children, safe homes, block patrols and public school crime prevention activities, can be used to make children safer.

Some recent exposes' about the sexual victimization of young children by day care employees have underscored the necessity of carefully evaluating a center before a child is entrusted to its custody. This appraisal is quite possible, even by a parent who has no experience in such matters, provided the suggestions contained in this chapter are followed, especially as they relate to personnel. Parents should visit the facility as often as possible and involve themselves in the affairs of the center once their child is enrolled.

In-home care, be it a housekeeper or babysitter, is an undertaking of great importance, and people must be willing to submit to a cursory background inquiry, as well as a personal interview. When a decision is made to hire someone, a written agreement that specifies their duties, responsibilities and benefits is recommended.

Children should be continually monitered by parents to ensure that they have not been the victims of crime, and to minimize the impact of assaults that might occur. Any signs of physical injury, behavioral quirks or even damage to clothing could mean trouble and must be investigated.

Latch key children are peculiarily vulnerable to crime and the fear of attack, so they should be the object of special training and continued supervision. Since the police are playing an increasingly more important role in protecting children, youngsters should be taught that enforcement officers are allies to be turned to in times of trouble, not adversaries.

While the question of whether a youngster should be permitted to attend rock concerts is something less than a major social issue, it does represent a continuing area of friction between parents and children. There are prudent ways of determining the risks involved in such attendance, using the guidelines previously discussed. As to the burning question of whether a youngster should be allowed to go to a rock concert, the answer is an unequivocal *maybe.*

The protection of children is more art than science. It involves close attention to detail, an on-going committment to security and an attempt to balance the need to protect against the realization that overprotection can retard a child's emotional growth. Pivitol to any security strategy is a relationship between parents and child that is based on trust, love, mutual respect and two-way communication. As luck would have it, this is not only a sound security practice, it is a pretty good way to raise kids.

BIBLIOGRAPHY

Burgess, Ann Wolbert, *The Sexual Victimization of Adolescents.* Washington D. C.: U. S. Government Printing Office, 1985.

Burgess, Ann Wolbert; A. Nicholas Groth; Lynda Lytle Holmstrom and Suzanne M. Sgroi, *Sexual Assault of Children and Adolescents.* Lexington, Mass.: D. C. Heath, 1978.

Chapman, Jane Roberts and Margaret Gates, ed., *The Victimization of Women.* Beverly Hills: Sage Publications, 1983.

Clearinghouse on Child Abuse and Neglect, Department of Health and Human Services. *Everything you Always Wanted to Know about Child Abuse and Neglect.* Washington D.C.: U. S. Department of Health and Human Services, 1983.

Johnson, Randy and Tana Johnson. "Are you Raising a Victim" in *FBI Law Enforcement Bulletin,* February, 1984.

King County Rape Relief Program, *He Told Me Not to Tell.* Renton, Washington: King County Rape Relief Program, 1979.

Lystad, Mary H., "Sexual Abuse in the Home: A Review of Literature" in *International Journal of Family Psychiatry,* Vol. 3, No. 1, pp. 3–31, 1982.

National Crime Prevention Council, "How to Protect Children." Washington, D.C.: U. S. Government Printing Office, 1985.

Schultz, Leroy G., ed., *The Sexual Victimology of Youth.* Springfield, ILL: Charles C Thomas, 1980.

Taylor, Carl S., *Rock Concerts: A Parent's Guide.* East Lansing, Michigan: 1985.

U. S. Department of Health and Human Services, "Child Sexual Abuse." Department of Health and Human Services, 1981.

_____, "A Parents Guide to Day Care", 1980.

_____, "Recruitment and Selection of Staff: A Guide for Managers of Preschool and Child Care Programs," 1985.

Chapter 7

FRAUD AND CON GAMES

If, as it is popularly believed, prostitution is the world's oldest "profession," then it is likely that the first prostitute was swindled out of her income by a con man, a member of the world's second oldest profession. The attempt by men to liberate people from their goods and currency through trickery or deceit dates back roughly to the development of goods and currency.

As early as the third decade of the Nineteenth Century, men travelled the nation's fledgling highway system selling tonics that promised to cure everything from skin problems to whooping cough. During the California Gold Rush, worthless mines were often sold to unsuspecting prospectors by owners who "salted" them with just enough gold nuggets to make the operation appear to be profitable. At the turn of the century, New York City immigrants were often introduced to the flow of city life by entrepreneurs who sold them, at very reasonable prices, full or partial ownership of a public utility called The Brooklyn Bridge, on which more than one enthusiastic owner tried to construct a toll booth.

While the preceding examples seem ridiculously transparent ways to separate a "client" from his or her money, variations of these schemes exist today. Indeed, even though con games and business frauds have taken on something of an air of sophistication, as computers, print and electronic media advertising and postal solicitation are now employed by swindlers, roughly eighty to ninety percent of all contemporary swindles are based on the tried and true tactics of snake oil salesmen, bogus gold mine owners and Brooklyn Bridge brokers.

Women, especially elderly women, are special targets for con men, who have developed their sales pitches to an art form. The success of these glib thieves is remarkable in light of the fact that most of their schemes have changed so little in the past one hundred years. Of course, the subject matter of their scams have been updated, but the actual nature of the swindles bears a close resemblence to schemes employed by long-dead counterparts, as anyone can attest to who has purchased their "miracle" weight loss cures (snake oil), bogus sight unseen vacation homes that turned out to be under water (The Brooklyn Bridge) and mail order sure-fire money making work at home projects that turned out to be expensive, time-consuming and worthless (salted gold mines).

What separates con games and fraud from most other crimes is that they almost always involve a victim who has willingly, perhaps even enthusiastically, entered into some sort of business relationship with the person who intends to steal from them. Unlike robbery, in which force is used, a con man employs persuasion, but to the same end as a robber. Most schemes involve short-cuts of some kind, short cuts to health, beauty, wealth or success. Some even play on the little larceny which resides in all but the most virtuous of us. While it is not possible to discuss every scheme that is practiced in America, the ones addressed in this chapter represent the most widely used scams that are aimed primarily at women.

The Con Artist, His Victim and His Lexicon

If a con man looked, spoke and acted like what he really is, then he would be forced out of the trade. There is a narrow gap between con man and convict, and swindlers do not wish to bridge that gap by engaging in a scam which is so transparent that even the most inexperienced people can see through it.

A real con man will pay scrupulous attention to his personal appearance. He will dress for his role painstakingly, whether it is in a business suit or work clothing. He will drive the appropriate car or truck, have the right type of identification, wear the proper jewelry and carry with him the correct tools, paperwork or accessories. In short, a swindler will precisely fit the part he has chosen to play. He may work alone or may have partners, depending on the con. Consider the description of con artists offered by The American Association of Retired People (AARP):

> The clever con artist is a good actor who disarms his victims with an affable 'nice guy' approach. But behind this friendly exterior is a shrewd psychologist who can isolate potential victims and break down their resistance to his proposals. Each conquest is a part of a game in which he must 'best' his fellow man.

Rarely are con men violent. They use their brains, wit, and a well-developed sense of timing. A swindler will try to cleverly disguise his fraud by making it appear so attractive that only a fool would pass it up.

The U. S. Postal Inspection Service succinctly summed up the problem when it warned consumers that

> . . . nobody would fall for a fraud if it looked like a fraud, right? So most of the time it looks like something else—a good deal, a business opportunity, a gift, or a chance to make a quick buck.

Any human being can be a candidate for victimization, even those who think they are too urbane to be conned. Nevertheless, most marks have common traits that make them more attractive targets than other people. On that subject, the AARP asserts that

> . . . many victims share certain characteristics. Often, but not always, they are older, female, and live alone. They are trusting of others— even strangers—and may need or desire supplemental income. Loneliness, willingness to help, and a sense of charity are characteristics a con artist will exploit to gain a victim's cooperation.

Since a con man is all but impossible to identify by appearance, and inasmuch as he softens his approach by making the con as attractive as possible, a potential victim must play close attention to the essentials of his proposal, not merely the euphumisms and cliches that are employed to disguise a scam. One has to look past the gloss and promises to evaluate a proposed business deal or investment. And when that close look is given, certain key words and phrases surface to place a person on notice that she may be on the verge of being a victim. Some of the most common terms and expressions employed by con artists include:

- A request for cash payment or for a check made out to a person not a business
- The need to act quickly or lose the deal
- A promise of quick riches considerably beyond the price of the deal
- The assertion that only a few people will be allowed to spend their money on the transaction and that you are one of the fortunate few
- A demand that the deal must be kept secret so that unauthorized people don't find out about it and cash in
- Guaranteed returns with very little or no work
- Extraordinary but impossible to validate examples of success stories
- An offer of free services or free gifts at an unspecified time after the deal is made

Classic Con Games

Some con games are almost as old as rocks. Nevertheless, they recur in basically the same form that they have always been practiced, against victims who should know better. Four classic schemes have been enshrined in the con artists hall of fame, and they merit attention here.

The Pidgeon Drop

A 74 year old widow is walking from the suburban grocery store she has frequented for decades to the home she has occupied alone in the six years since the death of her husband. Within a block of her house, she encounters a cleancut, breathless young man who exclaims that he is new in town and has just found an envelope stuffed with money, but without any identification. Since he is unfamiliar with the local community, he implores her to help him find the owner. He also asserts that if the owner cannot be located, the finder gets to keep the cash, which appears to be substantial. The man talks the widow into holding the money for him, but suggests that she should put up funds of her own as a show of good faith, since he fully intends to evenly split the proceeds with her if the police cannot locate the owner. The woman goes to the bank, withdraws a sum of cash, then gives it to the con man, who hands her what seems to be the cash-filled envelope. He departs to "call the police," and is never seen again. The woman's curiosity gets the better of her, so she opens the envelope prior to the arrival of the police, only to discover that it is filled with folded looseleaf paper.

The scheme which victimized the widow originated in China and is 1,000 years older than she is.

The Bank Examiner Con

In this scam, a person is usually contacted at home by telephone or when they are leaving or entering a bank. A man identifies himself as a bank official or examiner and explains that he suspects a bank employee of embezzlement but needs a long-time depositer to assist him in proving the allegation. The bank examiner asks his intended victim to withdraw a sum of money, usually thousands of dollars, so that he can mark it, then deposit it the following day to trap the dishonest employee, who is expected to pocket at least some of the cash. He dutifully explains that, without this cooperation, the dishonest worker will continue to steal. He promises that any loss of interest because of the customer's withdrawal will be more than made up by a grateful bank. The money is withdrawn, a very official looking receipt is issued for the funds, which, along with the examiner, are never seen again.

Missing Heir Fraud

This scheme is usually a form of mail fraud, in which a person receives a letter with an impressive logo from a business that purports to be an investigative or legal firm. The letter informs the recipient that a long lost relative has died, leaving a considerable inheritance, which the firm has been empowered to distribute. There are, however, modest expenses to be taken care of first, so the "heir" is asked to pay a small fee, almost always under one hundred dollars and sometimes as little as ten dollars, which most people feel is worth the risk to discover how much—or even whether—they have been left an unexpected bequeath. The con artists in this scheme rely on many small returns rather than one large payoff, and often rent a series of post office boxes to keep a step ahead of the law and irate "heirs."

The Obituary Scheme

The potential victim of an obituary scheme is usually a recently widowed woman who is contacted at home by a delivery man with a COD package for her deceased husband, whom the courier is "shocked" to hear has passed away. The package turns out to be a gift from the husband, who is supposed to have ordered it just before his death. The widow is so overcome with emotion that she pays an exhorbatant price for the item, which is usually an embossed bible or an article of personal or religious significance. The woman's name was, of course, obtained from the obituary column of a local newspaper and this stop may be only one of a dozen the con man will make that day.

Investment Fraud: Have I Got a Deal for You

Investment fraud has become a growth industry, one which rivals in scope and profits its legitimate counterparts. It is impossible to discuss here all the various schemes which plague investment-minded America, but some of the most notorious ones will be explained. It should be initially stated that there is no single vehicle for approaching potential investors, as bogus investment offers come by mail, through television, radio newspaper and magazine advertisements, by telephone solicitation and even in the person of door-to-door salespeople. Obviously, rip-off artists come at their targets from all directions and angles.

Work at Home Offers

How persuasive an advertisement must be to some householders to work profitably at home for a small investment, such as the following one which was carried in a recent magazine ad:

> Earn Up to $25,000 Per Year
> in your Leisure Time
> at Home
> No Special Skill Required
> Success Assured
> Minimal Investment

Investment in work at home scams can range from pocket money to a life savings. Most of the schemes involve some sort of manufacturing, some entail assembly or even plant growth; a few are offers to engage in telephone solicitation sales. One of the most dramatic recent examples of a work at home scheme that victimized legions of unsuspecting citizens was the so-called "mold scam."

The sales pitch was painstakingly simple: Grow mold in mason jars from curdled milk and sell it to a cosmetic company as a base product for cold cream. When the smoke had cleared, 25,000 people in twelve states had lost more than 50 million dollars on the purchase of kits ranging in price from 350 dollars to more than 2,500 dollars. Almost two million kits were purchased, meaning that even if there was a legitimate market for the product the supply so outstripped the demand that failure was all but assured. Some investors lost money that they could afford to lose; others were completely wiped out.

The Ponzi Scheme

Charles Ponzi, a Nineteenth Century Boston con man, invented an investment fraud that rested on a simple premise: promise a very big return on a very small investment. Ponzi's plan was to use the difference in international postal rates as a complex way of making profits by bartering stamps between nations. Investors were promised staggering profits. To Ponzi, however, the real money was not in trading stamps, but in the continuing growth in the number of investors so that he could use the "fees" from new enrollees to distribute "profits" to earlier investors, many of whom would then reinvest in the firm. When new investors dried up, the scheme naturally collapsed, since there had never been a market place in which stamps could be traded. Ponzi's swindle was a sort of pyramid operation which was destined to grow or die. It died, and his name became immortalized as the inventor of this recurring major con gam. During a recent three-year period, Americans lost almost 750 million dollars on variations of the original Ponzi operation, schemes that ranged from investments in an illegal—and fictional—ticket scalping syndicate to a plan to farm orchids at home.

Land Fraud

There is a booming business in land sales in America, most of which is legitimate but a portion of which is not. Land fraud usually involves either retirement property in warm climates, such as Arizona or Florida, or in vacation locales, some of which may be purported to be at or near ski areas, or on or by lakes, streams, rivers or the ocean.

The two primary mediums for land fraud advertisements are direct mail solicitation and newspaper or magazine ads. Most schemes begin with the purchase by a promoter of large tracts of cheap land which is more or less worthless acreage that can be bought in massive quantities at prices of 200 dollars an acre or less. The land is then subdivided into one, five or ten acre parcels and deeded for sale. The advertisement literature is prepared with colorful photos or artist rendings of attractive adjacent geographical features of the general region, features that have no relationship to the land offered for sale, which may be flat, waterless, scrub, or in the case of tropical parcels, inaccessible and partially submerged during rainy months. The sale will be made more attractive with low down payments and modest monthly installments.

Some classic land frauds have involved promises of planned communities: homes, roads, shopping centers, recreation facilities, sports opportunities, and the like, all of which will be ready "soon." Most people who have been defrauded in this way have never seen the land they contracted to buy. Some have, but after the purchase.

Ethical land sales operations are the norm; however, deals that sound too good to be true are probably neither good nor true. Retirement land can be one of the two or three most significant purchases of an individual's life and should be looked on as if a person were buying a new home or car, neither of which would be purchased sign unseen or without adequate investigation. If a land purchase is looked on as one would view a new home or even a used car, then it is likely that hype and high pressure tactics will not work in enticing a prospective buyer to snap up a "great deal." Remember, you would not buy a car by mail; why purchase land that way. Fraud can be avoided by seeing the land prior to sale, by asking people about it (e.g. realtors) who are not directly involved in its sale, by contacting the local or state agency empowered to regulate land sales, by consulting an attorney before signing a contract and by investigating the background and track record of the developer.

Precious Metals Sales

Two of the chief problems associated with the purchase of precious metals are: (1) the average person is not qualified to recognize whether a given metal is a bona fide precious commodity, or, if so, if it is of high or low quality; and (2) most fraudulent precious metal operations issue certificates of purchase, redeemable in gold or silver at a later date. For example, the failure some years ago of the International Gold Bullion Exchange, headquartered in Fort Lauderdale, Florida, resulted in hundreds of millions of dollars in losses to consumers, who had bought gold but had never received delivery of their purchases, which were supposed to be safely stored in the firm's vault, but were not, at least not in the quantities needed to supply all or a major portion of the investors.

In a sense, many fraudulent precious metals dealers are involved in a Ponzi-type operation in which the cash received from new investors can be used to buy enough gold to placate early investors. Things break down when growth declines or when some of the money that a firm has collected from clients is used in bad business investments rather than in metals purchases.

The purchase of precious metals, even from a reputable dealer, can be risky business since world political and economic conditions profoundly effect the prices of gold, silver and other metals. Nevertheless, the cost of these items is well known since there are daily price quotes in the financial sections of local newspapers. What may change is not the price of metals, but the broker's commission in buying and selling them. Furthermore, it is impossible to accurately gauge their worth without special knowledge or skill, inasmuch as age, condition, quality and availability of comparable coins play major roles in cost.

There is no foolproof way to making risk-free gold or silver purchases; however, some tips are recommended: know your dealer or someone who does "know him," only deal with people from reputable firms with a track record; investigate your purchase in advance; talk to someone who has dealt with the firm before; check with state regulatory agencies; if feasible, take delivery of the metals at or immediately after the purchase; do not buy the full quantity you want all at once—do it incrementally; avoid paying cash.

Home Improvements and Auto Repairs

Americans lose between five and six billion dollars every year to consumer fraud, with home improvement and auto repair ripoffs leading the way. The following case is a typical example of the problem.

She was a single woman with an active social life who liked to entertain friends at home. One day, she received in the mail an offer of a free air conditioning inspection. Since she thought that there was nothing to lose, she called the number on the circular to make an appointment for the next day. At precisely the time agreed to, a very amiable middle-aged man in blue coveralls with a large tool kit knocked on her door. He told the woman that the inspection would take about thirty minutes, so she could go about her business until he finished. In about a half-hour, he emerged from the air conditioner's storage closet with grave news. Her unit was about to break down and she was lucky he had found it in time. He pointed out small, pinhole leaks in the cooper tubing which served the unit. He indicated a circle of cold liquid on the wooden frame which surrounded the unit. He showed her several worn fittings. He scraped off several layers of rust from an ominous-looking coil. Luckily, they had found the trouble in time, so instead of replacing the unit, it could be repaired for $412.

The fraud here borders on the classic. While the woman was out of the room, the "repairman" tapered with the unit, puncturing cooper tubing with a miniature ice pick, removing good fittings and replacing them with well worn ones, squirting dark liquid about and attaching to a metal frame a rusty, completely useless but very official looking coil. The same approach is employed in frauds from furnace repair to roof maintenance, automobile body work to engine work.

Auto repair fraud can be a pernicious scheme, especially if it employs scare tactics designed to alarm people about safety equipment, such as brakes, or occurs on the open road where there is little choice but to make immediate repairs.

As in medicine, a second or third opinion is essential. Auto repairs, unless of an emergency nature, should also be deferred until other shops can evaluate the problem. When getting second or third opinions, the initial diagnosis and price estimate should never be shown to the other shops. Further, repair persons should be asked to point out and explain what they intend to do, and told to save replacement parts. All estimates should be precisely documented in writing and signed by a shop manager.

In auto repair fraud, specialized repairs seem to be among the most suspect, including such areas as:

Brakes
Transmissions
Air conditioners
Exhaust systems
Front ends

As far as fraudulent home repair is concerned, everything is fair game but there are some favorites of unscrupulous businesses, including:

Air conditioning and heating units
Roofing
Driveway repair and coating
Painting
Water heaters

Fraudulent products or additions to homes have also enjoyed brisk business as scam artists have cashed in on the energy conservation and sports and recreation crazes. Once again, there has been a focus by swindlers on selected products and additions, including:

Swimming pools

Solar heating

Room additions

Hot tubs and spas

Burglar alarms

Self-Improvement and Personal Enhancement Schemes

The American penchant for perfection has spawned a variety of fraudulent schemes designed to separate the vain, the upwardly mobile, the aging, the ambitious, the quasi-talented and the lonely from money many of them cannot afford to lose. These scams often blatantly promise everything, but deliver little or nothing, thereby contributing to a person's problem rather than its solution.

Some of the advertisements about products and services should, by their very nature, place consumers on notice that the offer is literally too good to be true: miracle weight loss without dieting or exercise; beauty products which for under $20 can dramatically transform even the most flawed individual; body building devices consisting of straps and pulleys that can create new bodies overnight; pills or creams that enhance sexual potency, clear up complexion, invigorate hair, quiet nerves, increase breast size, lengthen fingernails and improve circulations—shortcuts to personal improvement that can only really be achieved through more laborious means, if at all.

There are very few overnight mail order routes to success. While some products may be used as part of an overall improvement plan, it is folly to believe that pills and creams, for example, can perform wonders. But fraudulent products are only part of the overall problem.

Advertisements for services abound in the media. Home education courses which offer competencies in areas that require technical skills are often cruel hoaxes. How, for instance, can one learn how to perform a hands-on job by self-study.

"Vanity presses," which promise for a price to publish a book or song may be temporary ego-builders, but the likelihood that a writer will be "discovered" through this process is almost nonexistent.

The sale of products and services is generally an honest business; however, one should be immediately suspicious of any ad which seems to play on a person's vanity, ego, need for approval, quest for beauty or desire for a quick education. Human weakness and dissatisfaction with self or situation is a powerful motivator, one that has made entire generations of swindlers needlessly rich. Their creed can be effectively summed up in one phrase: "There is a client born every minute."

Business Fraud: Bait and Switch

In business, there may be a thin line between outright fraud and claims which mislead without violating the law. For example, if a room dehumidifier removes no dust, ragweed, cigarette smoke and pollen from indoor air, contrary to advertisements that it does, then clearly there is fraud. Yet, if a dehumidifier does filter such material from a room's environment but only ten percent of those pollutants, it may not constitute fraud in the legal sense, but no consumer will be saisfied by such a performance. So, business schemes aimed at extracting money from citizens for a service or product that does not do what it is supposed to is not only a case of omission or commission, it is a matter of degree.

One of the most widely practiced and long-standing corrupt business practices is the bait and switch operation, in which a product is advertised by a store at so low a price that it "baits" customers into coming in to buy it, only to encounter a salesman who attempts to sell them a more expensive item—"the switch"—since the bait product was only an illusion to generate customers.

According to an authority on the subject, the second part of this equation, "the switch" manifests itself in various ways, but is often revealed in one of the following ploys employed by a store:

1. A refusal to display or to show the customer the advertised product.
2. A salesman's criticism of the bait product (e.g. "I'm afraid that the picture is not real clear on a model that cheap.")
3. A disclosure that, in order to qualify for the bait item, it must either be bought in quantity or with another more expensive product—so-called "tie-in sales."
4. A warning that the product will be sold at the advertised price, but that delivery will take weeks or even months.
5. A surreptitious warning that the advertised product is defective, potentially dangerous or not appropriate for the intended use by a salesman who tries to convince his customer that the only reason the warning is being issued is for the citizen's protection.
6. Acceptance of a cash deposit on the bait item, only to later change the purchase and the statement to a higher priced product.

An Ounce of Prevention

In the case of most crimes, knowledge is the first step in a program of prevention. Understanding the nature and extent of household burglary, for example, allows one to then construct a reasonable strategy for lessening the probability of this form of victimization, based on practices, tactics and hardware that can be used to discourage burglars. In fraud and con games, however, knowledge *is* prevention, since awareness of the problem, in and of itself, is enough to puncture the plans of even the most sophisticated swindler.

Key to any attempt at avoiding fraud, is a change in perception. Instead of entering a transaction with the proverbial open-mind, a concept which has achieved the status of "mom" and "apple pie," it is recommended that a healthy skepticism be employed, a "prove it" attitude. Thus being closed-minded, demanding, a bit cynical, narrowly focused and skeptical, while vices in most endeavors, are virtues in business deals, retail purchases and repairs. Since so many scams attempt to create a psychological environment in which potential customers really want the advertised claims to be true, a dispassionate approach to sales by consumers is essential.

For every fraud or con game, there is a law enforcement agency empowered to investigate and act. In mail fraud, the U. S. Postal Inspection Service is the appropriate agency to contact. There should be no hesitation by a citizen about checking with these agencies in advance of a purchase to determine the track record of a business, or to report a fraud once it has been perpetrated. A local Chamber of Commerce, Better Business Bureau or Consumer Affairs Agency can also be turned to for advice or information.

So, knowledge of scams, a built in cynicism, a readiness to investigate all go a long way toward protecting consumers, who in the past have made more than willing targets for swindlers and unscrupulous business people. The stakes are large and deterrence is uncomplicated in short: Be a hard sell!

Conclusion

The most remarkable aspect of fraud and con games is how little they have changed over the generations, though the mediums for advertising them have kept pace with Twentieth Century America. Nevertheless, con artists still roam the land employing such classic swindles as the pidgeon drop and obituary schemes.

Investment frauds abound with work at home scams and land swindles leading the way in a country seemingly preoccupied with moonlighting and retirement planning.

Because of the technical aspects involved, home improvements and auto repair ripoffs may be among the most difficult frauds to prevent, especially if repairs and improvements are portrayed to consumers as emergencies.

Self-improvement schemes often appeal to the lonely, the upwardly mobile, the vain and the semi-talented. The success of many of the scams appeal to the hope and optimism that resides in most people.

In the area of business fraud, the bait and switch operation is probably the most widespread of all illicit sales practices. Unfortunately, businesses which in all other ways are legitimate often employ this tactic, which is as old as mass communications.

Knowledge of the essentials of fraud and con games is, by its nature, a form of prevention. Let the buyer beware is a key phrase, as consumers should assume a posture of enlightened skepticism in the face of sales pitches that may or may not be accurate.

BIBLIOGRAPHY

American Association of Retired Persons, "How to Spot a Con Artist." Wash: AARP, 1982.

Benson, Chris. "How Con Men Swindle Women Out of Their Money." *Ebony.* July, 1981.

Diggs, J. Frank. "How to Protect Yourself Against Latest Con Games." *U. S. News and World Report.* June 7, 1982.

Nimmons, David and Katherine Barrett. "Don't Be Conned!" *Ladies Home Journal.* November, 1982.

Moffett, Al. "The Pros and Their Con Games." *The Saturday Evening Post.* Jan/Feb, 1981.

Suthers, John W. and Gary L. Shupp. *Fraud and Deceit: How to Stop Being Ripped Off.* NY: Arco Publishing, 1982.

U. S. Postal Inspection Service., "A Consumer's Guide to Postal Crime Prevention." Wash: Postal Inspection Service, 1985.

Chapter 8

THE EMOTIONAL IMPACT OF CRIME

Two divorced women take their young children to an afternoon performance of the circus. They park in the public parking lot of the coliseum and walk to the main ticket window where they purchase tickets for the show, at which they spend a pleasant two hours. When they return to their car, they discover that someone has broken the vehicle's antenna, which lies bent and useless on the asphalt. It will cost 39 dollars to replace.

A single young woman meets an apparently reputable man at a popular lounge near her home. They chat for a time and seem to get along well. He asks for her telephone number, which she gives him. The following day he calls to ask her for a date. She accepts. On Friday evening, he picks her up at her apartment. They eat dinner at a fashionable restaurant, following which they go to a nightclub and dance, drink moderately and talk. He takes her home and asks if he can have a cup of coffee before he leaves. She agrees. Once inside, he becomes more amorous than she feels comfortable with at this stage of their relationship. She tries to resist his advances, but he will not let up. He forcibly rapes her, then leaves, promising to call again.

A legal secretary works late typing some important papers which are due to be filed in civil court the following day. She finishes at about 9:00 p.m., then takes the elevator from her office on the 26th floor of a downtown bank building to the fifth floor parking garage. She walks from the elevator to her car, at which she is startled by the sight of two disheveled young men who suddenly appear, seemingly out of nowhere. One grabs her purse and shoves her to the pavement. They both flee. She is not seriously injured. When the police arrive at the scene, they locate her purse on the next parking level, relatively intact, but with 23 dollars missing.

One way of measuring the impact of crime is to calculate the monetary losses which victims sustain. It makes a nice statistic, but tells so little of the real cost of criminal victimization that it is grossly misleading.

113

Perhaps the real, the profound impact of crime lies in the almost incalculable physical and emotional toll it exacts from people, influences which are easy to describe but difficult to measure.

Two of the above cases had an economic cost: one of 39 dollars, the other of 23 dollars. The remaining incident—the rape—entailed no apparent monetary loss. Nevertheless, to say that the total "cost" of the three criminal events was 62 dollars, is to gloss over the real tragedy of crime in America. Most everyone can identify with the anger and frustration the woman in the first case must have experienced in finding her antenna broken in a wanton, purposeless act of destruction. And what influence does such meanness have on children, such as hers and those of her companion. The rape in the second case resulted in no overt financial loss, but the devestating emotional scars on the victim, together with her need to submit to protracted therapeutic counseling certainly represents real "costs." The woman whose purse was snatched may or may not have required treatment for her injuries and to help her cope with the experience, but it would be a rare person indeed who did not encounter some lingering emotional difficulties because of the event, problems which can result in major modifications in life style.

Rarely are people "wiped-out" economically by what a criminal takes from them; yet they may well be "wiped out" emotionally or drained financially because of injuries sustained or psychological problems which had to be treated as a result of their victimization. It is a sad fact of life, but one which merits attention here.

On Coping with Crime

Any sensible woman will exhibit some kind of a reaction to a crime which has victimized her. The reaction will vary according to a number of factors, not the least of which are the nature of the crime and the degree of her involvement in it, but there will be an effect.

In the case of a vandalism to a home, the immediate reaction may be anger and exasperation, which is ephemeral. It is doubtful if there will be a long-term impact of any significance. Rape, however, will often have both immediate and lengthy consequences, in which a victim exhibits complex emotional side-effects that recur and may worsen over time. Even victims of property crimes, such as burglary, may show some of the signs that characterize interpersonal assault victims.

The point here is that it is not abnormal for a person who has suffered some loss at the hands of a criminal to react in ways that are atypical of their everyday behavior. In fact, those victims who show no outward reaction to their experiences may well be repressing symptoms that should be expressed. The goal of any crime victim must be to evaluate the effect of criminal intrusion on their lives and to determine how to best cope with problems associated with their encounter, even if that means counseling or other forms of treatment. Of all the crimes which victimize adult women, none is more disruptive than rape.

Rape Trauma Syndrome

The aftermath of rape can be devestating to a victim. Physical injuries sustained during a sexual attack may be painful, serious and a long time in healing. Damage may range from fractures, concussions, lacerations and contusions as a result of the battering a victim received, to physical symptoms in the area of the body which was the focus of the sexual attack, with the most common problems being vaginal discharge, burning sensations during urination, rectal bleeding, and both general and specific vaginal pain. It is likely that all but the most critical injuries will heal; however, there are psychological implications to somatic damage. As long as there is pain, irritation, marks or scars, they serve as a vivid reminder of the attack and make recovery more difficult. A permanent facial scar, for example, is a constant sign of the rape experience. Nonetheless, it is often the emotional effects of rape which have the more protracted implications. Elizabeth Stark, in a study of 2,000 women crime victims, found that sixteen percent of the women who had been raped had nervous breakdowns after their assault, while almost twenty percent attempted suicide.

The short and long-term impact of rape was ably documented by nursing professor, Ann Wolbert Burgess, and sociologist, Lynda Lytle Holmstrom, after a study of rape victims treated in the emergency room of a Boston public hospital. As a result of their work, Burgess and Holmstrom developed a concept which they called *The Rape Trauma Syndrome*, a framework for understanding the gravity of the rape experience, as well as the emotional consequences of victimization.

Rape is a traumatic and life-endangering encounter that results in a series of symptoms, the most pronounced of which is fear, an emotion that produces acute stress in victims. The rape trauma syndrome subdivides the emotional aftermath of rape into two phases: (1) *the acute stage;* and (2) *the long-term process.*

During the *acute stage,* a wide variety of emotions may be expressed, including shame, a sense of degredation, rage, a need for vengence and a feeling of culpability. The fear reaction is often extreme, as victims may for the first time in their lives dread death and serious injury. These reactions vary with a victim's age and background, her values and personality traits, and the gravity of the rape. Youthful, unmarried women are most often heavily impacted by sexual assault, because of the extent to which they feel guilt and shame. The acute stage begins immediately after the assault and continues for as long as a month.

Behavior which is atypical of a victim's normal way of acting surfaces during this first phase, and she may experience wide mood swings. Some women will talk incessantly about their assault; others will refuse to discuss it at all. In an effort to put the experience behind her, a victim may simply repress the urge to talk about her incident, hoping it will go away It may temporarily, but this strategy has a heavy price.

The *long-term process* is the intermediate and protracted reaction to rape. As in the acute stage, the nature, the extent and the depth of reactions vary with each victim, but there are some fairly uniform symptoms. *Traumatophobia,* a term first used to describe a soldier's response to combat, is a phobic reaction which also afflicts rape victims. In its simplest form, a phobia is an abnormal fear that has little basis in reality—an irrational dread. Specific post-rape phobias often relate to the place the rape occurred, the physical characteristics of the rapist or anything that reminds a victim of the crime. Phobias may be related to men in general, any type of sexual activity, certain odors or even colors. Examples of frequent phobic responses include: fear of being alone; fear of the indoors; fear of outdoor areas, such as parks; fear of crowds; fear of being in close proximity to people; sexually-related fears, and fear of men, which may take on specific shape, such as an aversion to men of the same race, or age or physical similarities of a rapist.

Some phobias may be very narrowly focused. For instance, a woman who was raped in the parking lot of a medium-sized private hospital became terrified of asphalt, and spent a good deal of her time trying to avoid walkways that were made of that material. Another woman who was abducted and sexually assaulted on a golf-course developed an antipathy to the smell of freshly cut grass. Reactions such as these are not at all unusual.

Nightmares are a common long-term rape reaction. Burgess and Holmstrom attributes two types of dreams to victims: one in which a woman is faced with a deadly or unpleasant confrontation but awakens before doing anything about it; and another in which she is able to master the confrontation, often in a violent way. The nightmares are progressive, meaning that for a time a victim may experience the first form, but will later progress to the second.

Outward behavioral cues can alert one to the effect that a sexual assault has had on a woman. The absence of signs, however, does not mean that there has been no significant emotional impact—quite the contrary. A woman who seems to be coping well with her ordeal may be merely delaying her reaction by disguising the emotional turmoil she is experiencing. The following chapter discusses some of the treatment strategies employed to help rape victims confront their problems. It is the authors' opinion that any woman who has been raped should seek professional help from a therapist who understands the phenomenon.

Robbery Reaction

A woman's victimization by robbery may be direct or indirect, as discussed in Chapter 4. Basically robbery with a woman as a victim occurs when she is present during a holdup of a business, such as a bank or convenience store; when she herself is heldup with a weapon, usually a handgun or knife; or when she is "strongarmed" or "mugged" by an attacker who through fear, threats or physical force makes her surrender personal property, almost always a purse or jewelry. Of all the crimes which target women, victims of this type of attack stand the best chance of being injured, sometimes very seriously.

As in rape, the more serious the injury, the greater the likelihood that fears associated with an attack will linger, especially if there is long-term or permanent scarring to remind victims of their ordeal. The well-known emotional consequences of sexual assault may cause women who have been raped to seek help from a therapist, but robbery victims will often ignore the psychological ramifications of their experience and focus exclusively on recovering from physical injuries, if any. Whereas a rape victim, regardless of how brutal the attack, almost always goes to the hospital for an examination and prophylactic measures, following which counseling is usually recommended by the hospital staff, a woman who is uninjured in a robbery or one who refuses treatment for minor injuries, will simply go her own way and ignore emotional problems which inevitably follow an attack. Robbery is a frightening experience, a crime which leaves its marks on women. For example, in the Stark study previously mentioned, almost twenty percent of all female victims of completed robbery had nervous breakdowns or either contemplated or attempted suicide following their attacks.

While rape is viewed by victims as a life threatening situation, many robbery victims who had been heldup at gunpoint described fears that their deaths were imminent. Ghastly nightmares resulted as the crime and bizarre versions of it became recurring dreams. Robbery victims often avoid sleep or find that they are unable to sleep because of their fear of nightmares. Sleep disorders, then, abound in victims.

Mugging or strongarmed robberies also have their effect. Phobias are often the outcome, with most fears directly related to the circumstances of the attack. A strongarm robbery in a parking lot may lead to fears of concrete, or parked cars or even parking lots in general. One woman who was knocked down while carrying groceries to her car, has recurring nightmares in slow motion of groceries—cans, boxes, fruit and vegetables—spilling crazily to the asphalt. In her attack, a plastic carton of milk broke, splashing milk on the parking surface. To her, the sight of spilled milk causes great distress and flashbacks to the assault.

Nighttime attacks are bad enough, and can carry with them a phobia of darkness. Women may simply become terrified of being in a public place at night. Daylight robberies can be even worse. For a time, one can avoid going out after dark, but a phobic reaction to daylight robbery may entail a fear of being alone in bright sunlight. Some of the most common phobias include fear of being alone, fear of people behind them, fear of sidewalks, fear of elevators or closed-in spaces, fear of teenage boys, fear of certain fabrics, fear of crowds and fear of public transportation.

The fear, anger and frustration caused by robbery usually causes victims to sharply change their lifestyles. These modifications are designed to help them avoid people, places and situations that are most associated with their attack. Without professional help, it is doubtful that phobias will pass, though they may be somewhat controlled. What usually occurs, however, is that phobic reactions control the victim, rather than the reverse.

The Violative Nature of Burglary

Classical burglary, in which someone surreptitiously enters a home to steal, then escapes with or without property after avoiding detection by either a householder or the authorities, is probably the most frightening of all "property" crimes. It violates one of the most sacred of all American institutions: the home, a setting where one should be assured of privacy, safety, comfort and a relative freedom from intrusion.

When a woman's home is burglarized, it convinces her that there is nowhere that she is safe. It also raises compelling questions in the mind of victims: Why me? Is someone watching me? Will he come back? When I come home will he be waiting? Has he looked at and handled my most personal possessions? What does he know about me? These queries haunt victims, causing them to alter the most fundamental aspects of their existence. In effect, many victims are frightened to be away from home, fearful of returning home and terrified to be at home alone, where every shadow, every noise, even the most routine ones, become crises.

Burglary is a violative crime. It violates one's most inviolably private place. The crime has been likened by some psychologists to rape because victims often feel as if they have been attacked and debased by a stranger. Whether one subscribes to this point of view or not, household burglary has an assaultive effect on victims, one with many of the stressful outcomes of physical assaults—fear, rage, frustration. And as in other attacks, these psychological problems must be confronted and overcome, preferably with professional help.

To walk through hallways and rooms in which a burglar has stood, or to open drawers that have been rifled by a thief, or to look at windows and doors that have been defeated by an intruder, is a great burden for a woman, especially if she lives alone or with small children. The depth of her emotional difficulty may be great and lingering. Many women make immediate efforts to relocate to another residence. Those who decide to remain, or for financial reasons must stay, often make major decorative changes—paint, wallpaper, etc.—to inhibit continuing recollection of the intrusion. It cannot be stated too emphatically that it is natural, even predictable, for a burglary victim to experience what to her may seem like irrational fears.

Childhood Victimization

One of the greatest concerns of parents is that their children will be sexually abused. But there are different types of sexual attacks and degrees of assault, making it difficult to generalize about the nature of a child's reaction to abuse. In some children, especially the very young, the experience will be evaluated by them on the basis of whether it was pleasurable or painful.

Factors which most influence the reaction of a sexually abused child are manifold. *First,* the relationship of the child to the attacker is important. The closer the relationship, the more trauma may be associated with the attack. All things being equal, assaults by total strangers are generally less traumatic than those by acquaintances or relatives. *Second,* the age and maturity level of the victim plays a major role in post-assault trauma. The more mature the victim, the greater the likelihood he or she will be equipped to cope with the ordeal. *Third,* the type of assault plays a crucial role in a child's reaction. The assault may be merely verbal or it may entail just touching, or it may involve hand-genital or oral-genital contact, or even attempted or completed penetration. Obviously, the more memorable the attack, the greater the emotional impact. *Fourth,* the degree of violence or force employed by an attacker represents an important factor in a child's reaction and eventual adjustment. *Fifth,* whether a sexual attack recurs over a period of time, and if so for how long, is a major determinent of the child's reaction.

Children can display a wide range of behavioral reactions to sexual attack, from profound disorders to minor eccentricities. Youngsters may also exhibit few outward symptoms, or at least no dramatic ones.

A characteristic of some assailants is to attempt to persuade a victim to tell no one about the attack, as if it is a shared secret, the disclosure of which is a breach of trust. Children who are taken in by this subterfuge usually experience internal conflict caused by their desire to inform parents versus the pledge of secrecy. There are two diverse ways that youngsters react to this dilemma: they may either act considerably older than they are, emulating adult behavior; or they may regress to behavior more typical of a younger child, perhaps even infantile. Any behavior outside the norm can be a tipoff to sexual abuse, such as a child who takes an inordinate number of baths or showers, or who scrubbed himself or herself unusually vigorously, or who brushes his or her teeth energetically and often, without instructions to do so.

While reactive behavior may range from the subtle to the pronounced, children often have trouble hiding their feelings. In a sense, younger children have not quite developed either the defense mechanisms or the avoidance behaviors associated with adulthood. So, if something is bothering them, it usually comes out in the form of observable responses, which may be tenuous but are there nonetheless.

The Complicating Role of Justice

When a criminal is arrested for the offense of larceny, burglary, robbery or sexual assault, the state cannot try him unless a victim testifies against him in court. In a property crime, the owner or custodian of the stolen items must identify them in order to prove that there was a loss and that the accused had no legal right to them. In an assaultive crime, a victim must explain in court the nature of the assault and identify the defendant as her attacker. This process, while essential, often complicates and extends the emotional trauma associated with victimization.

Criminal justice, as generations of attorneys can attest to, is an adversary process in which theoretically, two able trial lawyers do battle, within the framework of some procedural rules, to determine the guilt or innocence of a defendant. Unfortunately, witnesses are quite often the currency with which the state can prove its case, or by which an accused can purchase his freedom.

Criminal courts seem preoccupied with decorum. Judges are often disinclined to permit an attorney to yell at a witness, or to "badger," threaten or intimidate her. However, many experienced trial lawyers have learned to use a velvet glove in cross-examinations, a technique that consists of soft tones, ready smiles and knifelike questions, since a victim's description of her attack and attacker must usually be discredited by a defense attorney if his client is to have a chance at acquittal. So, a lawyer will bore in on "inconsistencies" in a victim's version of the attack in order to discredit her story. In rape cases and trials involving child victims, there are additional procedural protections to insulate (somewhat) witnesses from overzealous cross examinations. In other assaultive or property crimes, witnesses have no special protection.

It is ironic that the defendant in a criminal trial can—and does—refuse to submit to pre-trial depositions, but a witness will be forced to testify by deposition, which is not attended by judges and thus open for lawyer mischief. In Miami, for example, a six year old boy was deposed by a defense attorney named Jeffrey Samek in a child sexual abuse case, during which the lawyer said to the child: "I'm Frank's friend and I want to help Frank and I think you're lying. I don't think any of the things you've been saying about Frank are true. Do you know what a lie is . . . " When the boy denied lying, Samek twice ordered him to "Look at me." He closed with: "I think you've been lying to me . . . I don't think Frank ever did anything to you. Frank didn't do anything to you, did he?"

The criminal court process is slow and adversarial. The conviction of an accused defendant depends on whether a victim can persuasively discuss in open court* the essentials of her victimization. This experience can lengthen the ordeal of crime, while rekindling the fear many victims have tried so hard to dissolve. The American legal concept that a defendant has a right to face his accuser is a democratic principle of longstanding, but one which is traumatic indeed for victims.

Conclusion

The impact of crime goes far beyond the economic cost of criminal behavior. There is an emotional toll that criminals exact from their victims, one which may result in dramatic changes in behavior as well as modifications in life style. The extent to which a woman is affected by crime depends on the type of crime and the degree to which she is involved.

Both property and more personal offenses have emotional impact, with burglary, robbery and rape heading the list of crimes which lead to emotional reactions in victims. Rape especially has dire psychological implications for women.

The most widespread reaction to crime is fear, sometimes continuing over long periods of time. A variety of phobias may result and hinder a victim's ability to cope with her ordeal and to live a normal life. Child victims have special problems and their reactions to attack vary with a number of recognized factors, not the least of which are the severity and nature of the attack and their relationship to the attacker.

The criminal trial of a defendant accused of attacking a woman is an adversary proceeding which can complicate the emotional distress of crime victimization by forcing her to submit to cross examination that

---

*With some exceptions in cases of child victims.

may not be gently handled by a defense attorney intent on vigorously representing his client. A trial can be especially harrowing for child victims, who are afforded greater protections by courts than other witnesses, but who still are affected by the trial process.

BIBLIOGRAPHY

Berglas, Steven, "Why Did This Happen to Me." *Psychology Today,* February, 1985.

Burgess, Ann Wolbert, A. Nicholas Groth, Lynda Lytle Holmstrom and Suzanne M. Sgroi, *Sexual Assault of Children and Adolescents.* Lexington: D. C. Heath and Co., 1978.

Burgess, Ann Wolbert and Lynda Lytle Holmstrom, "Rape Trauma Syndrome" in *American Journal of Psychiatry* 131.9, Sept., 1974.

Fox, Sandra Sutherland and Donald J. Scherl. "Crisis Intervention with Victims of Rape" in *Social Work.* 17. Jan. 1972.

Frank, Ellen. "Psychological Reactions to Rape" in Testimony before the U. S. Senate Subcommittee on Juvenial Justice. April 24, 1985.

Hendricks, James E. "Criminal Justice Intervention with the Rape Victim" in *Journal of Police Science and Administration.* Vol II, No. 2, 1983.

Hicks, Dorothy J. "Rape: Sexual Assault" in *American Journal of Obstetrics and Gynecology.* Vol. 137, No. 8, August 1980.

Lawson, Judi and W. A. Hillix, "Coercion and Seduction in Robbery and Rape." *Psychology Today,* February, 1985.

Peters, Joseph J. "The Psychological Effects of Childhood Rape" in *World Journal of Psychosynthesis.* Vol. 6, No. 5, May, 1974.

Schultz, Leroy G., ed. *The Sexual Victimology of Youth.* Springfield, Ill: Charles C Thomas, Publisher, 1980.

Sgroi, Suzanne M. *Handbook of Clinical Intervention in Child Sexual Abuse.* Lexington: D. C. Heath, 1982.

Silver, Larry B. "Sexual Abuse of Children" in *Phenomenology and Treatment of Psychiatric Emergencies.* N.Y.: Spectrum Books, 1984.

Chapter 9

CIVIL LITIGATION BY VICTIMS

Although some might argue with the proposition that America is beset by difficulties, no one would disagree that it is also a society which makes available to its citizens a variety of remedies, one of which is becoming increasingly popular with women who have been victimized by crime: the civil suit. Lawsuits are neither appropriate nor feasible in all cases of crime victimization; but in a selected number of cases where the factual situations are right, litigation has proven to be an effective way of compensating women for the ordeals they have suffered.

Few suits are filed against the criminal who actually injured or damaged his victim, for two reasons: often the assailant is never caught; and if he is, it is doubtful that he has the resources to pay a damage award. Instead, suits are filed against the premises in which the crime occurred. These so-called "third party" suits—litigation against businesses, or even governments—are among the country's fastest growing types of civil actions, thanks to a groundbreaking incident, as well as a rapidly evolving body of case law which seems to be plaintiff-oriented.

Some years ago, singer Connie Francis was sexually-assaulted in a motel. She filed suit and won. The resultant publicity, as well as the extent of the money verdict, seemed to give people ideas, lawyers included. The race to trial was on, as victims—often women—of crimes—usually rape and robbery—filed suits against businesses of all types, particularly hotels and motels, apartment buildings, shopping centers, parking lots, retail stores, hospitals and lounges.

The underlying concept involved in the growth of this form of litigation, as well as the developing case law, is that a person or company which invites individuals to do business with them has a higher duty to protect these invitees than a non-business entity, such as a homeowner. The security provided need not be flawless, but it should be reasonable and consistent with community practices or industry standards. Further, if a business has undertaken a responsibility to provide security, even if the security provided exceeds all recognized standards, it must keep the

125

security program functioning properly or it may be held civilly account-able for defects which lead to victimization. A majority of this chapter contains actual crimes which resulted in litigation. First, a discussion of the civil court process.

Civil Court Procedure

Civil court procedures vary from state to state, and some suits may even be filed in the Federal District Courts, so it will be necessary to describe civil procedure in general. The litigation process formally begins when the plaintiff's attorney files with the court a complaint that contains a description of the alleged negligence and the damage which was sustained. Within a specified period of time, the defendant's attor-ney formally responds to those claims. The time between the filing of the suit and the trial (or shortly before the trial) is called the discovery process, during which each side tries, through deposions, interrogatories and other techniques, to find out as much about the other's case as possible in order to prepare for trial.

The plaintiff's attorney must prove two things at trial: that there was *negligence* on the defendant's part, and that the plaintiff was *damaged*, as a result. On the negligence issue, the nature of security-related litigation makes it necessary to conduct a good deal of pre-trial research.

Ordinarily, in order to show negligence by the defendant, it must be established that the crime which victimized a woman was *reasonably foreseeable* to the defendant. That is where the research comes in. The two generally accepted ways of determining foreseeability are to find out whether the premises involved is located in a high crime area, or if any crimes occurred on the property that were relatively similar to the one that injured the plaintiff. A police officer or an expert witness can testify to the first point, while crime statistics and police reports from local law enforcement authorities will be introduced to address the second.

The stronger the proof of prior criminal activity at the business, the greater the likelihood of a plaintiff's verdict. For instance, a woman who is badly beaten in a parking garage by would-be robbers will, if there were a half-dozen similar assaults in the same garage in the year before hers, have a better chance of proving negligence then if the garage had been crime free prior to her assault.

In concert with the foreseeability argument, the plaintiff will try to show that there was a lack of adequate security on the defendant premises and that had proper security been in place, the crime would have been prevented within a reasonable degree of certainty. Depending on the business being sued, security deficiencies may include a lack of guards, substandard lighting, defective locks, no access control or perimeter protection, door and window defects, to name some of the most prominent examples.

If the jury finds that there was negligence, it can award compensatory damages, a payment designed to compensate the victim for her experience. In cases where the jury wishes to punish the defendant because of a reckless disregard for the security of invitees, which is usually based on an excessive number of prior crimes as well as an absence of security, then it may grant punitive damages.

Cases Which Resulted in Civil Litigation

The remainder of this chapter consists of actual civil court cases, all but two of which resulted in plaintiff's verdicts ranging from $85,000 to $550,000. The two exceptions are incidents which at this writing were still awaiting trial. The cases were selected to represent examples of the variety of premises being sued by women and one is an illustration of suits involving child victims. The cases which follow are not concerned with the civil trials aspects of each matter; they are descriptions of the crimes which led to litigation. No names or specific locations are given in order to spare the victims, most of whom suffered lingering emotional problems as a result of their experiences, further distress.

Robbery at a Grocery Store

On a Saturday in mid-July, a married woman in her mid-thirties drove from her home in a quiet neighborhood on the outskirts of a large city to a store owned by a nationally known grocery chain. It was about 9:30 p.m., the store closed at 10:00 p.m. and she only needed a few items.

When she arrived at the store, which was located in a fashionable business district not known as a high crime area, she was able to park her station wagon directly in front of the store, which had a row of large plate glass windows that overlooked the parking lot. She was perhaps 25 feet from the automatic sliding doors. The lighting in the parking lot, while not state of the art, was adequate. She entered the store to shop. While she was shopping, a bagboy, who had just assisted a customer with her groceries, noticed what he later termed a "suspicious car" with two male passengers roaming the lot, but he did not call the police or notify anyone in the store. Seven minutes later, the woman walked from the store to her car.

She had two packages in her arms and a purse strapped to her shoulder. The groceries were light, so she carried them out herself. She walked down the sidewalk to her vehicle, turned into the space on the driver's side, held the groceries against the car with her body, then opened the rear door, which was between her and the store. The door slightly nudged a car in the parking space alongside.

As she placed her groceries in the station wagon, the "suspicious car" drove past the store entrance, stopped, backed up and parked behind the woman's auto so that the right rear door of the car was in line with the rear of the station wagon. A man got out on the passenger side while the driver kept the motor running. He walked down the narrow space between the woman's vehicle and the car parked next to it, confronted her and demanded her purse.

She was quite literally trapped in the narrow space between the open door of her station wagon and the assailant. Both grocery bags were now inside the wagon, along with her purse, which she and the thief grabbed simultaneously. A brief tug of war resulted, the strap on the handbag broke and the man pulled the purse free while the woman fell against the open door, then to the ground. The robber fired one shot from a gun he had pulled from his waistband, striking the woman in the abdomen. He and his partner fled as store personnel rushed to aid the wounded woman. Her wound was severe but she survived and her attacker was later apprehended, tried, convicted and sentenced to state prison, along with his accomplice.

While the store was in an attractive business district, and it was frequented by a rather affluent clientele, it had experienced problems with crime which belied its tranquil appearance and setting. In the 16 months prior to the shooting, the police had been called to the store 23 times. Many of the crimes they looked into were minor, such as vandalism; most involved burglary or theft. Some were quite serious and similar in nature to the robbery.

Over that 16 month period, four women's purses had been snatched from shopping carts inside the premises as they shopped. In each case, the thief ran from the store and avoided capture. On one occasion, a shoplifter stabbed an employee who tried to stop her from leaving the store with stolen meat. Four incidents which had taken place in the parking lot were the most serious customer-related crimes, three of which occurred within five months of the shooting.

In the first case, a man struck a woman in the face after they both had parked in the lot. He fled without taking anything and it is not known exactly why he attacked her. Within a month of that incident, a woman who exited the store with a handful of groceries was punched and knocked to the ground by a young man who grabbed her purse, ran to an awaiting car and escaped with two other men. Three months later, a woman who was walking through the parking lot had her purse stolen by an assailant who pushed her down and snatched it from her shoulder. Within a month of the shooting, another purse was stolen from a store customer while she locked her car. A man came up from behind, grabbed it and sprinted to a waiting car.

It seems that a pattern had developed at the store. Excluding the attack on the store employee, and excepting all other crimes, there were eight intruder-related attacks on customers within a year and a half. All victims were women, and a purse was taken in seven of the cases, three of which resulted in injuries. During that period of time the store added nothing in the way of security, even though other local stores in the same chain employed security guards or off-duty police officers.

Verdict: For the Plaintiff
Award: $350,000

Rape in an Apartment Complex

When the young woman awakened on the morning of August 18, 1981, to fix her roommate breakfast, there was no sign that she was on the verge of experiencing the greatest ordeal of her life. She worked as a convenience store clerk in the evening, and it was not easy to arise at 5:30 a.m. each morning to prepare breakfast, but she enjoyed it and her roommate was grateful.

They shared a second floor apartment in a suburban 422 unit complex located in four low rise buildings resting on the equivalent of three square blocks. While the premises were not lavish, there were open spaces and two swimming pools, which made it a comfortable place in which to live. Most of the occupants were young adults and although there was a high rate of turnover, the place had a consistent occupancy rate of 90 percent. Many residents were either blue collar workers or young professionals. A significant number were single parents, women who were trying to make a living and raise a family. The property located in a moderately high crime area, was patrolled by a security guard.

Shortly after breakfast, the woman's roommate went to work and she returned to bed, only to be awakened by a knock on the door. She asked who it was, and a male voice called for John. She replied that there was no John there. Without opening the door, she went back to bed. A short time later, she awoke to another sound. This time, a man was in her bedroom. He was wearing a handkerchief over his face and held a knife. She screamed twice, whereupon he put the knife to her throat and threatened to kill her if she screamed again or refused to cooperate. He bound her to the bed with a belt and shoe laces, then raped her, covered her eyes with white stockings and searched the apartment.

He was after money, but found none. When the bound woman told him that the only money she had in the house was bus fare, he beat her. For two hours he stayed in the apartment, though once he left for a brief time. The woman heard him leave a second time and she worked her way free. When he did not return she decided to escape, but was frightened that she might encounter him if she left by the front door. She went to the balcony off the bedroom and jumped from the second floor. She lay on the ground for about ten minutes, stunned from the jump. Eventually the police were called. She later discovered that the attacker had stolen her video recorder.

To say that the apartment complex had been troubled by crime would not be giving it enough credit. During the four years which preceeded the rape in this case, the police had been called to the place more than 400 times, calls that included 150 burglaries, 55 (non-sexual) assaults, 6 holdups and dozens of prowler reports. It was the sexual assaults, though, which represented the most dramatic, the most damaging and the most recurring problem. In the two years immediately prior to the attack, the following sexual assaults had occurred in the complex:

18 September 1979, 8:30 p.m. A woman is raped in an elevator by an assailant who had stopped it between floors.

28 September 1979, 6:30 a.m. A woman is raped in a first floor laundry room.

7 October 1979 A dazed woman who had been raped was found wandering around the halls. She could give little information on the suspect or the time the crime had occurred.

17 May 1980, 1:00 a.m. Another woman is raped in a first floor laundry room after she had been accosted in a hallway and dragged there.

30 May 1980, 2:30 p.m. A woman is assaulted then dragged into an elevator where she is raped.

25 June 1980 3:00 a.m. A man breaks into an apartment where he sexually assaults and terrorizes the occupants.

27 August 1980, 1:00 a.m. A man follows a woman through the hallway leading to her apartment, then forces her into a laundry room and rapes her.

5 September 1980, 10:30 p.m. Another woman is forced into and raped in a laundry room.

20 September 1980, 5:00 a.m. A woman is followed down a hallway, is forced outside the building and raped on a grassy area.

25 September 1980, 11:30 p.m. Another laundry rape.

May 1981 to September 1981 There are three more rapes which were not reported to the police, but which the security guard was aware of.

13 August 1981, 1:50 a.m. A man breaks-in an apartment and rapes the lone female occupant.

Fourteen rapes and over 200 felonies at the same complex.

> Outcome: A $300,000 out-of-court settlement
> with the apartment complex.
> A $750,000 verdict against the
> security firm.

A Convenience Store Murder

A young man drove to a nearby convenience store to pick up his brother-in-law, a clerk who was getting off-duty. He arrived early and decided to take a nap in his car. He dozed for about twenty minutes, during which time two armed men entered the store intent on robbing it. It was closing time, so no cash was available; the clerk had deposited it in a drop safe behind the counter. The robbers became agitated when they discovered this.

Just as they began to leave, the clerk's brother-in-law walked into the store, unaware of what was taking place. He and the two robbers reached the door at the same time. Words were exchanged. As the gunmen walked away, one turned, took aim and fatally shot the man. His wife, on behalf of herself and her daughter, sued the corporation which owned the store.

The store appeared to have violated recognized anti-robber standards in the industry: signs covered the windows, inhibiting surveillance from the street; the check-out counter was placed at an angle that practically hid it from outside view; there was a drop safe, but there was no sign on the door or window that warned potential robbers of limited cash on hand, meaning that the robbery was in progress before that fact was discovered. The store had been robbed five times in the past 18 months, considerably above the norm for convenience stores.

The case was settled for $100,000.

A Motel Rape

When the man, his wife and their six-year old son checked into the motel, it was supposed to be a stay which combined business with pleasure. It was a luxury inn in a resort area, to which the man had come for a job interview. The family planned to remain there for five days.

On the second morning of their stay, the woman took her son and went to the pool after her husband had left on business. Near lunchtime, they headed back toward the room, which was located on the second floor of the motel, a three story, 150 room facility which was in a low crime area. Just as they reached their room, they were accosted in the hallway by a man who pulled a gun and pushed the woman and her child inside. He tied the boy and his mother to the beds and ransacked the room. He then sexually assaulted the woman, who worked herself free when he left. She summoned management and the police, who arrived promptly.

There had been no previous rapes at the inn; however, there had been three robberies, 26 burglaries, two assaults and a dozen larcenies during the previous year. The motel formerly employed uniformed security personnel with guard dogs, but when the barking dogs disturbed sleeping guests, the service was discontinued and not replaced.

Although the police record of reported crime at the premises did not seem to be excessive, three interesting facts surfaced before the trial. First, a maid who had left her job in the past year told plaintiff's attorney that her husband made her quit because the place had become too dangerous to work in since the security service had been discontinued. Second, another maid said that employees were discouraged from calling the police, so there had been many more crimes at the motel than were reflected in police records. Third, a maid who had been on-duty during the day of the rape admitted that she had seen the assailant prior to the attack "acting suspiciously" on the third floor trying to look through peepholes on the room doors, but she did not tell management because they really did not like to hear about those kinds of problems.

Verdict: For the Plaintiff
Award: $150,000

A Molested Child

The apartment complex was a stark, 300 unit facility with five mid-rise buildings clustered on about five acres. Elevators and stairways served each floor, which had outside walkways that overlooked the parking lots. The rate of unoccupied apartments was consistently high.

Living in a two-bedroom unit on the third floor of building "B," one of the buildings which allowed children, was a seven year old girl and her parents, who tried to watch the youngster carefully because the neighborhood was a high crime area. On several occasions, the girl had been instructed by her parents not to talk to strangers and to only play on the landing adjacent to her front door.

On a late Sunday afternoon, the child was playing alone on the walkway in front of her apartment when a lone young man approached her and asked if she wanted to jump rope. She did. He told her that he had left his rope on the next floor, so she would have to accompany him there if she wanted to play. He led her downstairs, shoved her into a vacant apartment, and sexually molested her. She ran home afterwards and told her parents. The man, who was not a resident of the complex, was eventually arrested.

The crime rate of the neighborhood did not seem to have spread to the apartment complex. There had been a rape at the premises five-months earlier, but that had occurred as the result of an early morning burglary. During the year before the molestation, there had been only seven reported burglaries, not an excessive number for a complex the size of this one. Nevertheless, there were some other factors which contributed to the young girl's attack.

The apartment employed an unarmed security guard, who was on-duty when the girl had been assaulted. He had seen the assailant shortly before the incident, but did not challenge him because he believed the man was there to visit friends. The same guard had told management after the first rape that the property was simply too big for him to patrol alone. His recommendation for a second guard was refused.

Moreover, rather than locking the unoccupied apartments, they were either left completely open, or nailed shut. It was common knowledge that neighborhood youths had drug parties in those units. Management, in order to protect its property, removed all appliances when an apartment was vacated. Part of the security guard's duties were to go around and nail shut the doors which had been pried open the night before. Inasmuch as he considered this a futile chore, the guard only did it occasionally.

> Verdict: For the Plaintiff
> Award: $50,000 Compensatory Damages
> $500,000 Punitive Damages

Suing the Police for Rough Justice

The woman was accused of causing a disturbance at a popular restaurant in the nicest section of a moderate-sized city. When the police arrived, they arrested her for disorderly conduct. Inexplicably, officers told her female companion, who was also given the woman's purse, not to follow them to the police station.

When the woman and her captors reached police headquarters, a uniformed sergeant decided that instead of booking her they would issue her a citation if she signed a promise to appear in court. She did, and was released from custody. Somehow, without money or a ride, she had to get across town to her home. Her request to use a telephone was ignored. Officers thought her plea for a ride home was humerous. She left the station on foot, hoping she could flag down a taxi.

The police building was located in the highest crime area of the city, within sight of a strip of bars that had a reputation for violence. The bars closed at 2:00 a.m.; she left the station at 2:05 a.m. Within a block, she was kidnapped by two men, taken under a highway overpass and raped. After they abandoned her, she hailed a cab and went home.

She was angry, confused and disgusted by her experience. Mostly, she felt dirty, so she showered, scrubbing herself roughly. When finished, she sat for a long time before deciding that the police should be notified. When officers arrived, they were a bit skeptical of her story and visibly upset that she had showered, thereby ruining "evidence." When she asked to go to a hospital, they told her that she could do so after their investigation. First, they wanted to find the rape scene.

They loaded her into the rear of a paddy wagon and drove around until she found the general area of her assault. Next, they had her walk along the roadway in a light rain searching for the exact spot of the rape. When she found it, they returned to police headquarters, where she gave a formal statement. It was not until a day-shift police lieutenant, who had reported for work at 6:30 a.m., ordered one of his cars to transport her to a hospital, that she received medical assistance.

Verdict: For the Plaintiff
Award: $85,000

False Arrest for Shoplifting

This case involves a Latin woman who was suspected of shoplifting by security officers at a nationally-known discount store, and who was taken into custody even though there was no probable cause to do so. The most revealing account of the incident was given in a written statement taken from the woman afterward. It is reprinted below:

> Sometime late in the afternoon, I went to the department store and went to the washing machine department to check prices on a washer that I was interested (in). I went with my daughter who is 13 years old ... while I was looking at the washer, she went to the girls' department and was looking at some items. I met her there. She asked me if I would buy that, and I replied 'no' you have plenty of clothing. She left the articles and we both walked out of the store toward my car when a man come (sic) behind me, grabbed my arm, and told me to come with him. I became very nervous and asked him what was going on. My daughter translated what he was saying and she started to cry. The man took me into the store to a small room. On the way he told me that he was a security guard and displayed his badge. When I was in the room two more person (sic) come (sic) in who said they were the managers. Before I entered the room, he summoned a female employee who also came inside the room. The security guard told me that I had stolen, that he was going to have me arrested and he was going to call the police. I was in the room for about two and half hours. During that period of time the two managers were in and out. The security man left the room and the female employee left when an older female Spanish speaking employee entered and told me that the security guard or manager, I do not recall exactly which one, had sent her to search me for stolen items. The first thing she did was check my purse, and

thereafter, she told me to take off my clothing, including my shoes and my underwear. I proceeded to undress completely. The woman told me that she felt very bad, but that she had to do it because the manager had told her to do so. While I was nude the woman told me to turn around several times and to bend forward so she could see me completely. She told me to get dressed as she did not find anything on me. She opened the door and the two managers and the security man were standing outside. At that time my son had been called by my daughter. The female employee who searched me told the men that I did not have anything on me. They all were very apologetic and told me we could leave. At that time I was very nervous and upset and all I wanted to do was leave the store, so I told my son and daughter let's go as soon as possible. My husband wanted me to make a complaint but I was too upset and embarrassed and I wanted to put that behind me.

Verdict: This case is awaiting trial.

Rape in a Luxury Condominium

When the middle-aged couple purchased their ground-floor condominium in a large resort community, they anticipated using it seasonally, since they were about five years from retirement. They had selected their unit carefully so that they had a view of the sea and could enjoy its cool breezes. The complex, much of which was still under construction, was in a very low crime area.

The community employed one security guard on the midnight shift, stationed in a gatehouse that controlled access into the development. Every so often, he also walked the grounds, which meant that there was no access control when he made his rounds. During the first year of its existence, not one single crime had occurred on the grounds.

The back exit of the couple's unit was served by a sliding glass door that led from the living room to a small, unscreened back patio. The door had two locks: the standard thumb latch that locked it in the closed position; and a sliding vertical bolt fastened to the top side of the sliding door. This bolt slid upward into a hole drilled in the frame to provide extra security when the door was closed. Additionally, another hole was drilled into the frame so that the door could be opened six inches and the bolt slid upward into the frame. This allowed one to sleep with the sliding glass door slightly open, but theoretically "locked" in place.

The only thing that held the vertical bolt in place when the sliding door was in the six-inch open position, was the slight tension that was created when the bolt rested against the outer rim of the drilled hole. The greater the wear, and the more the bolt was used, the less tension existed. The idea might have worked if the bolt had been held in place by a spring, but it was not. If the door was shaken, the tension on the bolt was relieved, and it fell out of the hole, leaving the door unsecured.

One evening, while her husband was away, the woman decided to sleep with the sliding glass door in the partly open position and the vertical bolt in place. While she slept, a prowler saw the door slightly ajar. He quietly slipped into the patio to examine it and reached in to feel what was holding the door in place. In doing so, he accidentally shook the door and the bolt slipped down, freeing the door, which he silently pushed open. He entered the unit, raped the woman, then left, later to be captured.

This case was settled for $350,000

Conclusion

Women who have been victimized because of a lack or absence of security now have a method of achieving at least a measure of justice, even if their assailants are not apprehended. However, civil suits and the threat of them are fulfilling another function. Litigation has persuaded some and complelled others in business to take a hard look at their vulnerability to crime, often for the first time, as a way of ensuring that they are protected against large, highly publicized civil damage awards. As such, civil suits filed by women have had the effect, often unplanned, of protecting other women from the negligence of business which histori- cally exhibited little concern for the security of invitees. In effect, civil litigation has become an instrument of reform.

INDEX

Fear
    effects control on, 70
    forms of child's fear, 89
    in acute stage rape trauma syndrome,
      116, 122
    programs to reduce, 71
    social control perspective, 69–70
    victimization perspective, 69, 70
Fingerprint/photograph program for
    children, 81
Fleming, Jennifer Baker, 33
Flynn, Errol, 52
Fox, Sandra Sutherland, 123
Francis, Connie, 125
Frank, Ellen, 123
Fraud, 99–112 (*see also* Con games)

G

Garofolo, J,, 7
Gates, Margaret, 96
Genovese, Kitty, 69
Goldberg, Steven, 27
Gottfredson, M., 6, 7
    lifestyle/exposure model of
      victimization, 6–7
Grant, Cary, 51, 52
Greenberg, 59, 64
Groth, A. Nicholas, 21, 22, 23, 27, 96, 123

H

Hendricks, James E., 123
Hicks, Dorothy J., 27, 123
Hillix, W. A., 123
Hindeland, M., 7
Holmstrom, Lynda Lytle, 96, 115, 117, 123
Home improvements scheme, 107–109,
    112
    case illustration, 107–108
    prevention of con, 108
    types frauds most common, 108–109
Household burglary, 49–57
    as preventable, 57
    attempted forcible entry, 49
    categories of, 49
    characteristics of burglar, 51–53
      professional burglar, 52, 57

      relationship to victim, 52–53, 56–57
      typical burglar, 52
    conclusion, 56–57
    forcible entry, 49
    incidence, 49–50, 56
    items stolen, 54, 57
    potential violence during, 55–56, 57
      incidence, 56
    profile of burglary in America, 49–50
    seasonable variations, 50, 56
    time of occurence, 50, 56
    tools of burglary, 53–54
      illegal tools, 53
    unlawful entry without force, 49, 50–51,
      57
      indirect entry, 51
      victim responsibility, 51, 57
    woman's reaction to, 119

I

Informal social control
    basis, 64
    conclusions, 67–68
    defensible space and, 68
    definition, 64–65
    factors in formation and cohesiveness,
      66–67
    importance of, 65–66, 68–69
    influence on serious crime, 67, 70–71
    intervention in crimes, 69
    organizational structure, 65
      table, 65
Investment fraud, 103–104, 112

J

Jacobs, 61
Jaffe, Natalie, 30, 48
Johnson, Randy, 96
Johnson, Tana, 96

K

Kanin, Eugene J., 13, 27
Kempe, C. Henry, 34
Klaus, Patsy A., 27, 57